Lacanian Psychoanalysis between the Child and the Other

Lacanian Psychoanalysis between the Child and the Other explores what topology can contribute to clinical work with children, emphasizing that psychoanalytic listening goes beyond the individuals who attend a session. This kind of listening does not seek for what is hidden inside; rather it seeks to create a continuous topological transformation, with topology regarded as the most sophisticated way in which structure, structuring and playing can be thought.

Using Lacan's theoretical framework, the book provides a new perspective on working with children, re-examining fundamental Lacanian concepts such as structure, subject, lack, Other, clinic and, of course, child itself. It charts how time and space are knitted together for children in psychoanalysis, and how a Lacanian approach can enable clinical practitioners and researchers to venture into cultures of childhood, helping them conceptualize and intervene in the process of knitting and unknotting.

The book will be of interest to psychoanalytic child clinicians in practice and training, as well as researchers in the field of child psychoanalysis.

Liora Stavchansky, PhD, psychoanalyst. She was born in Mexico City. Her practice is distributed between the psychoanalytic clinic and teaching at several universities, institutions and groups. Her research interests relate to childhood, infancy, subjectivity and writing topics as well as psychoanalysis. She is a member of Escuela de la Letra Psicoanalítica (ESLEP, México). She has published a number of psychoanalytic books in Mexico and Argentina.

Lacanian Psychoanalysis between the Child and the Other

Exploring the Cultures of Childhood

Liora Stavchansky

Routledge
Taylor & Francis Group

LONDON AND NEW YORK

First published 2019
by Routledge
2 Park Square, Milton Park, Abingdon, Oxon OX14 4RN

and by Routledge
711 Third Avenue, New York, NY 10017

Routledge is an imprint of the Taylor & Francis Group, an informa business

English Edition © 2019 Liora Stavchansky

© 2012, Paradiso editores, S.A. de C.V.

British Library Cataloguing-in-Publication Data
A catalogue record for this book is available from the British
Library

Library of Congress Cataloging-in-Publication Data
A catalog record for this book has been requested

ISBN: 978-0-367-00126-1 (hbk)
ISBN: 978-0-367-00127-8 (pbk)
ISBN: 978-0-429-44440-1 (ebk)

Typeset in Times New Roman
by Apex CoVantage, LLC

Contents

Acknowledgments   vii
Foreword by Ian Parker   ix

Introduction: perspective: the unfolding of a clinic   1

1 About psychoanalysis and other stories   13

2 The infantile and the child in Freudian theory   33

3 The Lacanian subject: notes for considering the place and
   function of the child in psychoanalysis   57

4 Language in analytical listening with children   73

5 Toward a topological articulation with the clinical praxis   98

6 What is a child-specter in psychoanalytical clinic?   122

Acknowledgments

I would like to thank Alejandra Del Ángel and Omar Espinosa Cisneros, because their work on this translation made the book possible. Also, I would like to thank Ian Parker for his introductory notes. Lastly, I would like to dedicate this book to Nicolás and Alexa for their existence weaves the fabric of life.

Foreword

This book is about time and space, about the way time and space are knotted together for the child in psychoanalysis, and about how a Lacanian approach to the child as subject can enable clinical practitioners as well as researchers to venture into cultures of childhood, giving them the possibility to conceptualize and intervene in the process of knitting and unknotting. This implies that some detailed theoretical work is needed to unhook psychoanalysis from the temporal parameters by which is defined in the popular imagination. These form the ideological matrix of banalized representations of psychoanalysis, most importantly those anchored in the idea that 'infancy' and then 'childhood' are chronological stages that precede adulthood, the later position being privileged and deemed as a superior vantage point from what has gone before.

In contrast, Liora Stavchansky shows us how Giorgio Agamben and Alain Badiou, among others, enrich psychoanalytic practice with children. Unhooking psychoanalysis from these temporal parameters is prelude to the innovative later chapters which bring space to the fore, and then we see how childhood functions topologically as an 'object of fantasy' as Lacan puts it, even as a 'fourth knot' in the Borromean triple circle of Lacan's later writing. This is where we also appreciate, by way of theoretical discussion that will be quite new to child psychoanalysts in the English-speaking world and through intriguing accounts of clinical case work with children, how important it is to reflect on the way that the peculiar time of childhood intersects with the time of the clinic.

So, *Lacanian Psychoanalysis between the Child and the Other* shifts focus from the register of chronological time as the culturally dominant frame for understanding 'the child' to that different kind of space that provokes fantasies about beings who are in some ways so familiar to us adults and in other ways so different. Actually, there are two different kinds of space conjured into being in this marvelous book. The first kind of space is the space of childhood as such, and we can refer to it 'as such' now at this point in history because it has been sedimented as a distinctive separate domain of existence, as if it were always there, available for the human subject to become who he is. We are reminded, however, that this 'child' is, as Stavchansky puts it, 'marked by the Other of history', and about how Agamben's argument is invoked to emphasize the point that the very 'infancy' that seems to define the pre-history of this child is itself not at all chronologically prior but is *constructed*.

The figure of the child haunts popular imagination as a place of lost inno-cence, increasingly today as the victim of adult predation, and it is worth reminding ourselves that this innocent child is the historically constituted flip-side of a child that, at the time Freud was elaborating the seduction theory as antecedent to psychoanalysis, was viewed as willful and deceptive. The potent semiotic link between children and fairies that is explored toward the end of this book was even once upon a time configured with a world of more frightful hobgoblins. The point is that, whether they are seen as untrustworthy or font of truth, 'children' were quite late in human history divided off from other human subjects and expected to live in a world of their own before eventually and necessarily abandoning it and joining the rest of us.

Today this child as an object of our fantasy is much more than the site of tenderness that Sándor Ferenczi would contrast with adulthood as a site of passion in a 'confusion of tongues' that would, in a normative developmen-tal and clinical sequence, eventuate in the properly confined delights of the genital drive. The game of misunderstanding that Stavchansky describes in her case studies is infused with fantasies about the child not only as desiring and desirable, but as positioned in Western culture both as commodity and as target of incitement to commodity fetishism. The child is reified, turned into a thing to be bought and sold, with cross-border adoption and trafficking as but two instances of this commodification, and it has become one of the objects of advertising, present not only in the representations of desirable goods – a mode of being that bears fruit in the image of the child as accessory in celeb-rity culture – but also as quintessential consumer in its own right. It is here that the discourse of child rights becomes so easily elided with the rights of the child to participate in consumer culture as an active agent and as prompt to their parents to also consume more. The child romanticized as other, if not at the same time the uncanny reminder of who we once were, inflects the popular psychoanalytic representation of it as the core and precursor of our being as desirous subject such that it becomes the site of trauma.

This is why it is so important that we are reminded in this book that 'infancy' and the 'child' function as signifiers that lack signification; their apparent full-ness of being is but an illusion, and we need an authentically psychoanalytic account, that which again Lacan began to provide for us, to truly comprehend that the idea that there is a substantive center inside the self is something that itself is illusory. We are reminded that Freud 'decentralized' the unconscious unveiling that there is no center around which language revolves and through which the subject communicates to others, and that in place of this illusion there is a void or lack. The task of the child is to reinstate this lack, a task which she repeatedly fails to accomplish, and which is at the heart of the clinical case examples that are knitted together for us in this book. In that way the child's singularity is knitted together inside the clinic and, crucially, *between* the sessions through its own particular kind of language which Lacan termed 'lalangue'.

The Lacanian rediscovery of the looping back of time so that what appears to be chronologically prior is created as such, after the event, '*nachträglich*', has implications not only for our understanding of 'trauma', but also for our understanding of the world today in a time of psychoanalysis, a time when psychoanalytic reasoning is one of the materially effective signifying systems for constructing child subjectivities as well as for constructing adult subjectivity in relation to children.

There is a second kind of space that is also important for us in our task of reading this book, for it is not only 'childhood' that has been created as culturally potent otherness to us today. We live in a world segregated in such a way that the English-speaking world is constructed in relation to other far away cultures in which, it sometimes seems, there is something strange and even incomprehensible about what it means to be a subject. This book was first published in Spanish in Mexico by Paradiso editores, and some of the clinical case examples speak not only of the singularity of the child but also of their cultural location, in some cases even as existing in sites of transition between cultures themselves, for example negotiating lives in Spain and Mexico.

One thing this book brings home to us in the English-speaking world is once again that while psychoanalysis is all around us here, in the implicit conceptual substructure of television make-over and radio self-help programs as well as in novels and films which rely on notions of 'trauma' – a reflexive interiority of self and unconscious processes that are amenable to interpretation in order to make narrative sense to us – this is nothing in comparison to how it is in Mexico and other parts of Latin America. There, psychoanalysis is not only the implicit resource for the construction of subjectivity, and therefore for our ideas about what children are, but forms the explicit topic of discussion, at the very least among those whose children will eventually engage in clinic work.

And, yes, there is then something strange and incomprehensible to English-speaking psychoanalysts about this attention to subjectivity, if not also to the actual subjectivity it engenders. The dominant currents of psychoanalysis are there Lacanian or at the very least infused with discussion of what Lacan has to say about them, and this makes this book into something very valuable for us to learn from. We see from the theoretical articulation of concepts from Lacan's work how it is that other cultural and critical theorists could come to play a key role in the understanding of what is happening inside the psychoanalytic clinic. And then we learn something about our own cultural reference points for the kinds of Freudian and post-Freudian theory that have been so powerful in framing our clinical work in child psychoanalysis. Stavchansky provides a series of reflections which are respectful and illuminating for practitioners here who have been schooled in the work of Anna Freud, Melanie Klein or Donald Winnicott. In this way the book operates as a link with another world where there is another language into which children are inducted and come to understand themselves.

Lacanian Psychoanalysis between the Child and the Other is exemplary, then, in the way it addresses a number of different dimensions of psychoanalytic theory and practice that bear upon the way we understand and work with children. In each dimension we are 'decentered', just as Freud decentered the unconscious to open up a form of work which attends to the symbolic coordinates of the subject. That attention to the symbolic coordinates enables us also to take some distance from the imaginary lures in clinical work (a peculiarity of countertransference in work with children, for example, in which we are invited to connect once again with who we once were) and then to know something better of what we are up against when we stumble across the real, the real of the body and the real of another being divided from us in the construction of gender and sexuality, for example, divided by the very language that seems to bring us together.

There is a social dimension in which we are decentered from the interior world of the individual child (a reductive fantasy of isolated and romanticized selfhood) to include the child in the world of the family and to include the family in a wider set of discourses and practices which render them into objects of the clinical gaze. There is a cultural dimension in which we are decentered from the closed and self-contained model of 'the child' (a fantasy which universalizes childhood at the very same moment as it occludes the different kinds of actually existing childhood in the world today) to see this culture as one among others in which we learn from those other cultures. There is a historical dimension in which we are decentered from our own particular time (a fantasy which encourages an arrogant dismissal of other times as mere prequel to our own) to reflect upon the historicity of our own clinical practice and conceptual reference points such that time does then become the substance of which we are made. And there is an ethical dimension in which we are decentered from reigning moral precepts (a fantasy of normative 'development' which pretends to tell us what we should adapt ourselves to so to become good adults) to engage with the child in analysis as *subject*.

Stavchansky shows us how the child is rendered as 'other', how we are positioned as 'other' to the child, and how our clinical practice knits the child and other in a relation to each other, a relation that does not pretend to be harmonious, that does not lock the two in a temporal narrative, but locates the subject somewhere between the two, that questions the time of the child and situates it in relation to a quite different kind of topological space.

Ian Parker
Manchester Psychoanalytic Matrix

Introduction

Perspective: the unfolding of a clinic

I slip between words and silence, in the place where the letter left trace of what is to be written . . . the place in which history begins.

It is my purpose to begin this book with questions about the psychoanalytical praxis such as the following: why does psychoanalysis use topology in the work with children? Is it possible to think of child psychoanalysis from a topological perspective? Throughout Lacan's seminars another kind of writing takes place, a writing that lies in a commitment to read Lacan *with* Freud. Not only is this writing produced mathematically, it is also produced in the presence of the clinic, a clinic of the signifier that includes the existence of the body. The dimension of the body I refer to is not a biological one, it is rather the dimension that results from the interjection between the real, the symbolic and the imaginary.

If we intend to answer these questions, we need to have a way to read the clinic, a way in which topology enables psychoanalysts to work with discourse. A subjective structure can be considered from topology, for it provides a better access to the (real) structure of space than Euclidean or bi-dimensional geometries. It is through topology that we can understand the nature of the real since it allows to locate the unconscious in a stature that lacks substance or a mere biological understanding of the body. Through topology the unconscious emerges in the fractures of discourse, in the gaps that exist between utterances and enunciation, which leave aside the universality of time and its rhythm.

Topology is not a mere literary resource nor a whim. Lacanian topology resides in the 'necessary' that is opposed to the 'contingent', allowing a clinic to be read from another perspective. Freud created an interpretation (*Deutung*) that untangled the obsessive or hysterical symptoms. With topology, Lacan produced an interpretation that is rooted in the castration complex. It is here that a cut, pivotal part of structure, enables the listening of the nonsense that appears in the analysand's discourse.

Knitting a clinic: between the child and the Other

Certainly, this title functions as a name or as a master-signifier; however, once the writing is finished, this name acquires a new shape, it becomes a *knit* that reorganizes the whole text. It is likely that this statement appears contradictory and blurry; nevertheless, it shows how difficult it is to 'finish' writing. The title of this book evokes a flow that can be transported to theoretical space, without ignoring the clinical consequences that result from theory.

The intermediate space the word 'between' introduces is not intended to add ambiguity to the clinical praxis. Some psychoanalytic approaches attempt to produce clinical effects only *inside* the psychoanalytical space. Contrary to this clinical method, Lacan stated that analysis is a process that is produced *between* sessions. For him, an analysis does not depend on continuity nor a chronological sequence of sessions; rather, he believed that each session can also be what interrupts continuity, produces a fracture, an interval or a distance from everyday activities or from the boredom of life. In other words, it is in the succession of intervals or scissions where a psychoanalytical process takes place, producing the most important clinical consequences.

To talk about psychoanalysis is to recognize that its clinic has as method the construction of a knit that begins specifically by its writing regarding the knitting of its letters, silences and words. However, this clinic has been defined as a "talking cure" (Freud, 1905d), in the sense that when we speak, we always produce a new texture also reflected in the writing composition. *Lacanian Psychoanalysis between the Child and the Other* refers precisely to this knitting, where enquiries get knotted with enunciations and statements producing the effect in *lalengua*. And, what also gets to be recognized is that when we speak we always say something more, less or different than what we desire. Here is where resides the possibility of creation and interpretation. From a Lacanian approach, writing is what modifies the relationship between the subject and the Other. A relationship which will be inscribed into the Other, transforming the anxiety of living into a symptom (Saettele, 2005, p. 92) sustained by the social peers. Therefore, *Lacanian Psychoanalysis between the Child and the Other* is the result of the intersection between primordial signifiers that slide between the text. Signifiers as structure, subject, lack, child, Other, *objet petit a*, the infantile and clinic. And, it's through these that we can grasp the distance that exists with the possibility itself of producing something new: an act.

This project has emerged from *between* the clinic and its ties. Concepts such as 'the infantile', 'childhood', 'infancy' and 'the child' are not new to psychoanalysis. However, Lacan's theoretical framework, based on the Freudian proposition, enables us to think and read from a different perspective not only the clinic with children, but also the concepts mentioned above.

It is not my intention to exhaust this matter; rather, I hope to establish the differences between these concepts. *I want to provide the reader with theoretical elements that allow him or her to view clinical work, specifically the psychoanalytical clinic with children, from a different perspective, one that is based on Lacan's theories, which do not fall far from Freud's framework.*

Even though the relationship that cuts across the child, infancy and the infantile is kept throughout this writing, it is important to clarify that for this book, I seek to emphasize one of Lacan's pivotal ideas for approaching 'the child'. The 'Mirror Stage' becomes the road that leads Lacan to unveil the history that precedes a subject. This history reveals that drives limit discourse; however, they do not limit the body. The 'Mirror Stage', far from being a mere experience in the life of a child, is the basis for the structuring of a subject, a structuring that is the paradigm of the articulation between the imaginary and the symbolic. Not only is the 'Mirror Stage' a structuring event for a subject, it is also the matrix by which future relationships will be established. This is the reason why drives cannot exist without a defense against them, a cut that functions as a wall that permits a discursive unfolding in psychoanalysis.

To better understand these ideas, we cannot ignore Freud's trajectory in infantile sexuality or in the psychosexual stages. We must emphasize the importance that Freud placed on the infantile, for this became equivalent to the unconscious. For Freud, "The unconscious of psychic life *is* the infantile" (Freud, 1916–1917). Therefore, Lacan's return to the Freudian framework produces a specific reading of this notion of 'the infantile'.

It is also necessary to realize that this text does not attempt to invent new concepts. *This text is an invitation to follow in the traditions of Freud and Lacan to create new ways in which the psychoanalytical clinic with children can be read.* It also seeks to reflect on the ties of what is sustained, listened and written in the psychoanalytical work with children. These ties allow an articulation of Lacan's most relevant ideas on topology. In other words, I intend to open a door to formulate questions about topology and its contribution to the clinical work with children. I also emphasize that psychoanalytical listening goes beyond the people who attend a session, such as the child, his parents, relatives and teachers. This kind of listening does not see what is hidden inside; rather, it seeks to create a continuous topological transformation (Lacan, 2009a).[1] Topology is the most sophisticated way in which structure, structuring and playing can be understood.

In Lacan's first seminar, *Freud's Papers on Technique*, we can read his position on psychoanalysis in the commentary that he made about Melanie Klein's clinical case 'Dick'. One of Lacan's arguments pointed out that the analysis of a discourse must be based on the primacy of the symbolic order, in its articulation with the real and the imaginary. Lacan asserted in this seminar that the problem concerning us resides in the articulation between the symbolic and the imaginary in the constitution of the real (Lacan, 1982). The Oedipal dimension, as outlined by Freud, introduces the castration complex. Lacan believed that what is common to all human beings is, in fact, that we are structured through the gap the castration complex opens (Lacan, 1982).

Here, the tragedy of Sophocles (*Oedipus the King*) is transformed from a narrative into a structure, a transformation that has consequences for the way in which Lacan understands the father as an operating function in structure. In other words, there is a change that moves from Freud's *Totem and Taboo* and *Moses and Monotheism* to Lacan's concepts of structure such as are found in the Name-of-the-Father, the four discourses and the formulas of sexuation.

To better articulate this approach, I will recall Lacan's words regarding "The Individual Myth of the Neurotic", where we can see his structural thinking even in his earliest work:

> We do not ignore that we were born from words and from that simple moment in which our parents laid together. The words of the Matchmaker also play a genesic role that will be reflected on the unconscious of a subject; that is to say, it will be reflected on his symptoms, on the illness that speaks, on the hollow, and if I may; on the physiological weakness that allows it to be integrated in that word.
>
> (Lacan, 2009b, p. 89)

Lacan's words, along with what we have just mentioned, take us to the central idea of this book: *The child appears there where the real of sex, the symbolic articulation of signifiers and the imaginary of its signification (experienced as sense or meaning) are knot together, so the child is born as a subject in discourse and revels itself in that discursive gap where the biological body remains extracted.*

The most relevant clinical consequence of this approach is that a symptom becomes the word itself; it becomes the revelation of the discursive limit of a subject. The subject suffers his symptoms in his own flesh; however, these are not part of his conscious discourse (Lacan, 2009b).

If the symptom is the word that insists on being listened to, then the psychoanalytical device is where this word acquires a place. Psychoanalysis, for Lacan, is a means of recognizing the function that the subject assumes in the order of symbolic relations, an order that extends to all human relationships and whose core is the Oedipus complex itself (Lacan, 1982).

In this way, the relationship between the psychoanalytical theory and the clinical praxis with children is, in every case, problematic. One of these issues is related to the listening of the subject that *says*, listening that the child sustains. This is the reason why there is a growing effort to thoroughly understand what a Lacanian clinic with children would entail. Numerous clinic spaces base their work on the 'application' of a theory to their praxis. Only a few pause to reflect on the theory that proves the implications of this theory for a clinical practice with children.[2]

It is important to understand that this project has gone through various stages (Peusner, 2006) which enables us to think about the clinic and the child from another perspective, a perspective that flows out of the Lacanian framework.[3] A child does not lie on the couch, yet he possesses the stature of a subject, for he has a place in the history of his family, a place which results from a weave made of desires. The 'subject of desire' operates in the history of his parents, from where it knits its own history.

Here resides the structural perspective of the subject proposed by Lacan. It is through words, silences, babblings, drawings and playing that the subject always *says* something. To better understand this matter, let us refer to Victor Lunger, who stated that discourse operates by virtue of what the patient specifically says and does not say in a session. Discourse for psychoanalysis operates through language and more precisely, through *lalangue*. *Lalangue* is what reveals the social ties of a subject (Lunger, 2005).

Not only does the subject enounce in analysis, it is also affected by enunciation. Utterances and enunciation are the components of a subjective dimension. It is in this dimension that the signifier and the *objet petit a* as remnant operate in discourse. Lacan asserted that dissymmetry is what characterizes relations; in fact, dissymmetry is what produces a residue (Lacan, 1982).

It is important to remember that a structure possesses a remnant; therefore, the articulation among the imaginary, the symbolic and the real directs the way in which an analyst thinks of the clinical work with children. The psychoanalyst signals the utterances of the child in a subjective field that enables the emergence of the relationship between the child and the Other. In analysis, the child places the psychoanalyst in the position of the Other, as someone who knows about him just as a teacher would. I believe that because of the influence that Lacan's thinking has had on the clinic, it is of fundamental importance to understand the consequences of his triad in the psychoanalytical work with children.

The dimension of language appears in the clinic cutting through the child. A child, regardless of his age, is always spoken by his own history, one that is marked by the 'Other of History'. History takes place as consequence of retroactivity, a time that reveals that language is what occurs between two parties in the relationship and articulation of signifiers. The radicalism of this notion lies in the fact that there is a point that can never be historicized. Lacan called this point 'the real'. Therefore, language belongs to the field of the Other. It is in this field that a subject emerges *between* two signifiers; signification appears as a sanction that comes from the Other. This function of language produces as its effect that, in the analytical space, a subject always says more, says less or says something different from what was intended. Lacan stated that the analytic experience lies in these ambiguities of language. He believed that these so-called ambiguities are the very jewels of language, solely based on the symbolic. However, the symbolic proves to be insufficient when a subject intends to express something, for the subject always says more than what was intended to say (Lacan, 1982).

The psychoanalyst serves a function that enables the production of subjectivity. It is because a subject is produced through the psychoanalytical listening that the analysand listens to what he has uttered rather than to the enunciation itself, an enunciation that is forgotten after being uttered (Lacan, 1984). The psychoanalyst, in the place of the Other as 'subject-supposed-to-know', allows a sort of reading, writing and punctuation to take place in discourse.

It is through this path that unprecedented ideas have been found. If the child is observed as a mere result of evolution, we miss the opportunity to consider the place that the child has in the chain of signifiers. However, if the child is read from a reformulation of evolutive processes, where the symbolic traces cut through the body (age), then the child (subject) appears in the intersections of the imaginary, the symbolic and the real. This intersection allows us to think of the child as hollow, for it is what is left from the subtraction of the three registers. As has been said, *the child is born in the knot that lies between the real of sexuality, the articulation of the signifiers and its imaginary signification.*

The psychoanalyst *reads* the symptoms that this articulation produces. For Lacan, the symptom of the child responds to the symptom of the whole family structure. The symptom can reveal a truth about the relationship of a couple (Lacan, 2005). He also believed that in the relationship that exists between symptoms and words, the symptom itself is word. The symptom is a word, for it resides in concrete discourse within the concrete limits of the subject. According to Lacan, the subject suffers in his own flesh from what goes beyond his consciousness and discourse (Lacan, 2009b).

As the analysand speaks through his symptom, the psychoanalyst reads and signals with his or her intervention. This is the subjective field in which the imaginary, the symbolic and the real reveal the relationship between a subject with the Other, a relationship that appears in words. The structuring function of language allows the *knotting* of this structure. The function of the resulting knot is based on the topological relationship that the elements have in a structure. It is in the field of the signifier that discourse loses contingence and continuum to enable the appearance of the signifiers. What results from this loss is the *objet petit a*; this appears as a residue that lies in the interval between signifiers. Psychoanalysis, therefore, does not intend to achieve completeness or harmony. Rather, it insists on revealing the impossibility that inhabits words, for they can never fully express desire (Lacan, 1999). Even though words mediate the relationship between the subject and the others through social ties, it is never sufficient. Lacan also asserts that something about discourse falls as residue. For him, psychoanalysis works with this residue that results from discourse. It is based on this understanding of residue that he stated that "the unconscious is structured as language", a structure that is revealed through the topology of knots and graphs.

It is from this concept of the subject that *topos* unfolds. For Freud, *topos* is where psychical processes reside, while for Lacan, *topos* provides an articulation. We can say that in the chain of signifiers, the child produces a hole in the Other's body, a hole that enables the union of anatomy with the chain of signifiers. As we have discussed, a Lacanian approach to the clinic with children leads to different ways of thinking, directing and intervening in psychoanalysis. For Lacan: "In the intervals of the discourse of the Other, there emerges in the experience of the child something that is radically mappable, namely, *He is saying this to me, but what does he want?*" (Lacan, 1987, p. 222).

The child that we refer to here is one that transits through the phallic or Oedipal stage, as well as the oral and the anal stages and the Oedipus complex. For Freud, the child has a polymorphously perverse disposition; this is to say that the child directs his sexual desires to any object in a disorganized and undifferentiated way. The child, therefore, lacks a sexual identity. His sexual desires move from a state of latency to their awakening during puberty. Freud's approach emphasizes the importance of drives from which the whole concept of sexuality deepens. The concept of drive shows that these drives flow against instinct. For Freud, the child, as opposed to the adult, inhabits an undifferentiated sexuality that is directed to change the goal of a drive. Child sexuality is oriented toward a non-sexual end, to sublimation. This is why we must think of perversion as an inhibition within the constitution of a subject, rather than as a state (Freud, 1905e).

The importance of the phallic or Oedipal stage is that in it 'the lack' is constituted. This is the primordial condition for the structuring of a subject. The subject is inscribed in the phallic function through the desire of the mother. Therefore, it is through the desire of a phallus that a mother allows the subject to take the place of desire. This approach follows Freud's formula 'child = phallus', a formula that shows the residue of a mythical unity. One of the questions that results from this work has to do with the relationship that exists between the polymorphously perverse disposition and the concepts of desire and drive.

If we depart from the Freudian perspective that sexuality is driven by pleasure rather than by a reproductive end, we can say that human sexuality is perverse and therefore, perversion resides at the core of all human sexuality. Because human beings access sexuality from the very beginning of their lives in a perverse way, pleasure will always be sought beyond mere reproduction. In *Three Essays on the Theory of Sexuality*, Freud described perversion as a deviation of the sexual act, a deviation that is directed to achieve sexual pleasure (Freud, 1905d); he also incorporates in his theory the relationship between desire and perversion, as well as the relationship between 'the polymorphous' and the drives.

If we synthesize the above, we can say that at certain times, the child is homologous to the structure of perversion, for it is only in the imaginary where the child can reveal the lack of his mother, understood as the Other. However, this lack is not inscribed in the unconscious. In perversion the lack can be assumed through the imaginary but not through the symbolic. In the case of neurosis, the lack is assumed through the symbolic, which is precisely what psychoanalysis intends to achieve.

A polymorphous perverse child who is going through the phallic stage will disavow the lack of the Other, its castration. He believes that his mother lacks a phallus but this lack is not inscribed. Thus, the perverse does not accept the trauma that castration and loss produce. The child denies pain and trauma; however, he attempts to capture the traumatic through his drawings and playing. The child takes a position in speech where he sustains the enounced, but he also finds himself in a quandary because there is no way for him to 'know himself', his own 'I'.

As we have mentioned, it is in the 'Mirror Stage' that the subject is captured by his own image. Here, the ego emerges through an identificatory process in which he assumes the reflection of the image as being his own. Lacan shows how at this time the ego is the product of ignorance because the ego is alienated in the image of the Other.

This specular time introduces the order of the imaginary, an order that by means of the mirror enables the emergence of the symbolic, for it is the adult who takes the child and holds him or her in front of the mirror. When the child assumes the image reflected in the mirror as his or her own, he or she turns to the adult, as the Other, seeking the affirmation that the image belongs to him or her. The child sees his or her own unified image, an image that is complete, and he or she also affirms the presence of the adult as the Other of the symbolic. However, the Other leads the child to realize that the image that he or she sees is false, an event that fills him or her with anxiety. This experience introduces the desire for completeness in the child. It is through this very experience that the lack will be inscribed in subjectivity.

We can now see the distance that exists between structure and development, between the subject and the child, a distance that has important repercussions for the way in which our clinical work is conceived. A Lacanian orientation leads to a particular way of intervening. Intervention now lies in structure rather than in phenomena. This is why psychoanalysis is closer to structuralism than to phenomenology.

Freud believed that the child, with its polymorphously perverse disposition, is organized through sexual desire, an approach that results in the primacy of the drives. By the time the child directs his sexual desire to his mother, he is also introduced to a perverse relationship with her. In this relationship the child's desire moves without the child realizing it. The flow of the child's desire is directed to his parents and it is they who will take the child as a symptom, a phallus or a specter,[4] after which the child may or may not fulfill the function of becoming a polymorphous perverse.

Summarizing, the main idea of this work is that *by not assuming the lack, the child disavows it and will attempt to re-establish it; however, he inevitably fails to re-establish this lack. It is through his words, drawings, playing, and also through his symptoms that he expresses this failure, one to which the analyst listens in the psychoanalytic space.*[5] These attempts open the possibility for a child to inscribe the lack in the unconscious, from which a neurotic structure results. In other words, *both child and adult deal with the lack: the difference between them lies in their discourse.*

The child does not realize that he is continuously being moved by the lack that inhabits his structure, a lack that also takes him as a phallus. One can read in our clinical work how the child affects the real, how the real affects the child and how he is unable to recognize this. In the psychoanalytical work with adults, the subject can realize there is a movement that takes place in his psychical structure; he realizes that the real emerges is an impossibility. An illustration of this is the impossibility that some people have in being able to plan long-term projects when they are close to death.

One of the hypotheses that informs this work is that the child organizes his discourse through his fantasy (imaginary) and his utterances (symbolic). However, this signifying frame also affects the real by changing the coordinates of the psychical structure. In contrast, the adult's desire is what moves him and also leads him to assume the lack, assuming a symbolic castration. Analysis is a clear example of this assumption. In analysis, when an adult talks about the death of someone close to him, he can formulate questions about his own life using words. However, he constantly finds himself in the impossibility of recovering through speech, for his speech leads him to an encounter with the impossible (real) of death. Now we understand that the adult is aware of the movements that take place in his analysis; his questions and associations evidence that these movements have occurred.

There is a clear difference between the way an adult speaks and takes responsibility for his analysis and how the child does the same. Can we think of this difference without referencing a developmental approach? If these are structural differences, does it mean that there is one structure for an adult and another one for a child? It is a fact that in the clinical setting, the position children and adults occupy is different, but does this mean that so are their structures? Or from a clinical perspective, is the same structure treated differently depending on the age of the patient? If the psychoanalyst takes a different place regardless of structure, is it because he responds to social conventions in which parents, teachers or family members tend to do so? If the latter occurs, how does it affect transference or clinical interventions? Can social conventions affect structure? We can see how these questions merit serious consideration in future projects.

In psychoanalysis with children we can see how the child imagines and symbolizes the lack without acknowledging it. A clinical illustration can help us understand how the previous statement takes place. Not so long ago, a child named Tomás arrived at my consultation room. Tomás was five years old, and he came to my office with his mother. During the first session, his mother interrupted to tell him that his father had just died. She said, "Your daddy is now in heaven with your grandma. . . . Do you remember that he told you he was going to travel? Your daddy went on a long trip and he's not coming back". Tomás answered sadly, "Oh . . . my daddy died; now I can't play Wii at his house anymore. . . ." It is important to note that Tomás's parents did not live together. Tomás's mother answered, "You can play Wii in our house, my love". I remained silent while this shocking conversation was taking place. I was extremely surprised by what was happening. Tomás was able to enunciate that his father was dead (the real), but he immediately started to talk about something else to displace his pain as a way to seek comfort. This event shows how the child cannot account for the lack in the symbolic; as a result, he is also unable to account for the lack in analysis. The child does not sustain the lack; it is the psychoanalyst who sustains it by asking questions that the child cannot formulate.

This leads us to think that there are different ways to treat the formations of the unconscious. The child cannot form questions about his symptoms, slips of the tongue or dreams. The child plays with the equivocal; he even laughs when these mistakes appear. He plays with language but fails to question these formations. For the adult, the formations of the unconscious become enigmatic, and thus, he is able to question them.

It is of fundamental importance to emphasize that the articulation of the real, the imaginary and the symbolic affects the way in which the psychoanalyst listens to the child in the psychoanalytical work. This work is guided by the effects that the articulation of the registers has on the child. However, there is one question left before closing this introduction: what is a child for Lacanian psychoanalysis? It seems as if this question has a simple answer, but Lacan answers by stating that the child is the only *objet petit a*. For Lacan, there is no other source for the infantile because the child is the only *objet petit a*—it is 'the child' who contains the desire of the Other (Lacan, 1955).[6]

Throughout this book we will learn that not only is the child located in structure as an *objet petit a*, but he is also located in structure as a subject, regardless of his age or maturity. We can assert that psychoanalysis seeks to find the dimension of desire in the child. As we have seen, it was Freud who changed the way we thought about infantile sexuality. Now, we consider the effect of the drives as part of sexuality. Lacan showed us that the subject cannot be understood by the mere imaginary. The subject for Lacan goes beyond the gaze that is set upon him. Finally, this work intends to raise awareness of a clinic that grants the child a subjective position, a clinic that seeks to act in the fissures produced by speech.

Notes

1 Lacan states that the unconscious is that part of concrete discourse which, in terms of being transindividual, is missing from a subject's possibility to re-establish a continuum in his conscious discourse.

2 When we use the adjective "Lacanian", we are referring to a specific way to study or think about the clinic. The Lacanian method enables us to understand that interventions are based on a technique that does not produce dialogues or anecdotes. This technique does not seek to treat patients based on observations or imaginary guidelines. On the contrary, psychoanalysis is aimed at the emergence of words and at the symbolic. The analyst listens to each patient without previous knowledge that might come as formulae or techniques used for interpretation or interventions such as those used to transfer from one ego to another ego. Psychoanalysis aims at the three registers and at the variability in the length of the sessions. A *Lacanian* clinic therefore, seeks to listen to the history of an analysand as a text, as a writing, rather than as a means to recover the patient´s memories.

3 It is also important to mention that throughout the three years that this project has lasted, there have been many important changes that oscillate from the interest in studying the clinic with children as poetry, to the intention of understanding the relationship that this clinic has with poetry, mathems and philosophy.

4 We mean symptom, phallus or specter as "positions" that the child can occupy in a structure.

5 These attempts fail because they intend to re-establish the lack. The failure of a structure is precisely that which moves a subject. The movement takes place not to make it complete but to evidence the failure of a structure through speech. In the case of children, this failure emerges in drawings, playing, words and symptoms.

6 How does Lacan go from the *objet petit a* to the one who desires? Lacan (2005) mentions that the symptom of the child responds to the symptom of the family structure. The child, then, is what represents truth about his parents. The child can be captured by his parent's fantasy because there is a distance between identification with the ideal of the ego and the mother´s desire. Therefore, if truth reveals the unconscious, then the child becomes the object for his mother, functioning only to reveal the truth about her object. The child in this position fails to distance himself from his mother.

Bibliography

Freud, S. (1905d/1953). *Three Essays on the Theory of Sexuality. S. E., 7*. London: Hogarth.

Freud, S. (1905e/1953). *Fragment of an Analysis of a Case of Histeria. S. E., 7*. London: Hogarth.

Freud, S. (1916–1917/1953). *A General Introduction to Psychoanalysis*. Conference XIII: Archaic Remnants and Infantilism in the Dream. *S. E., 15*. London: Hogarth.

Lacan, J. (2003). *El Seminario. Libro 14. La Lógica del Fantasma*. Buenos Aires: GAMA Producción Gráficas SRL.

Lacan, J. (1982). *El Seminario. Libro 1. Los escritos técnicos de Freud*. Buenos Aires: Paidós.

Lacan, J. (1984). *L'Étourdit. Escansión 1*. Buenos Aires: Paidós.

Lacan J. (1987). *El Seminario. Libro 11. Los Cuatro Conceptos Fundamentales del Psicoanálisis*. Buenos Aires: Paidós.

Lacan, J. (1999). *El Seminario. Libro 5. Las formaciones del inconsciente*. Buenos Aires: Paidós.

Lacan, J. (2005). *Dos Notas Sobre el Niño. Intervenciones y Textos 2*. Buenos Aires: Manantial.

Lacan, J. (2009a). Función y Campo de la palabra y el lenguaje en psicoanálisis. *Escritos 1*. México: Siglo XXI.

Lacan, J. (2009b). *El Mito Individual del Neurótico*. Buenos Aires: Paidós.

Lunger, V. (2005). El Discurso y *Die Verneinung*. In Benjamín Domb, Norberto Ferreyra, Roberto Harari, Víctor Lunger, Hugo Levin and Isidoro Vegh. *Seminario de lectura de Los Escritos Técnicos de Freud de Jacques Lacan*. Buenos Aires: Letra Viva.

Peusner, P. (2006). *Fundamentos de la Clínica Lacaniana con Niños*. Buenos Aires: Letra Viva.

Saettelle, H. (2005). *Palabra y Silencio en Psicoanálisis*. México: UAM-Xochimilco.

Chapter 1

About psychoanalysis and other stories

History is inscribed in the body . . . in the words of a non-existing reality and in the silence of an inhabited time.

Scraps of theory from child psychoanalysis

Once upon a time there was a boy who feared horses, his name was Little Hans. A phobia, a psychoanalyst would say. This boy's father took him with a man who indirectly crafted a land of fantasies, myths, legends, stories . . . and a little bit of adventure. This childhood land might be the place where our hero and some opaque shape of this boy would meet and the debate will start.

The discussion about the clinical practice that takes children as analysands has filled bookshelves for a long time. Even from 1937 in *Moses and Monotheism*, Freud would say that psychoanalysis produces a 'historical truth', and he also would insist on restoring the plots and illusions of which the child has always been part. Ever since that time, Freud pointed out that the fundamental psychical operation located in a weave of past relations is where the child becomes a subject. This movement allows the child to get involved in desire by inhabiting and being inhabited by it, hence taking a place; a historical one.

By historical, we shall not understand a relativism of the social outcome (social constructions or conditions) or a factual history of social happenings. When Freud speaks of historical truth, what he means is what Lacan would formalize in terms of structure. Structure is diagonal to the individual and the social, as well as to the objective and the subjective. The historical truth is a question regarding the complicated place that the child occupies within a genealogical fabric that has a structural nature. If historical truth is a question concerning a place within structure, then its time is logic, not chronologic; it responds to anticipation and retroactivity within a structure. Following Freud, it is under this structure and temporality that the historical truth and its possible interventions emerge.

Freud saw Hans only once, so it was literally the father who conducted the treatment. Hans's father had sent Freud notes about his first observations, making a contribution to the theories of infantile sexuality. He also confessed to Freud his difficulty in facing the enigmas that his son presented.

According to Freud, psychoanalysts are faced with impossibility when applying the psychoanalytical method to children due to the fact that a child is not yet accountable for what he or she does (his or her acts) or what the child says (enounces) in the psychoanalytical device. Most often, the parents are the ones who want their child to begin therapy since they are concerned with the behavior of the child, but not precisely about the child himself or herself. This is why the child cannot quite face his own history in the same way an adult would, even though his history is not without difficulty or shifts. It gets clearer if we consider that to Freud transference was essential to conduct a psychoanalytical treatment; however, this concept became more complex with the introduction of positive and negative transference. Negative transference is considered to be resistance, while positive transference moves the treatment forward. In this respect, Lacan did not agree with the notion of transference in terms of negative or positive.

Until then, the problem with Freudian psychoanalysis laid with the place that the psychoanalyst held in the complicated transference of the child, because it was the parents, and not the child, who requested treatment. If we look for responsibility within psychoanalysis and we ask the child, "what brings you here?", the answer we get is: "My parents".[1]

Initially, Freud considered that the only possible way to direct the treatment with children was if the father and the psychoanalyst became the same person. Years after the case of Little Hans was published in 1908, Freud would change this assertion. Later on Melanie Klein, without publicly admitting it, would include among her first cases the analysis of her own three children. She was granted a degree as a psychoanalyst after presenting her third case. Beyond these anecdotes, the complexity lies in listening to the subject, who is also a child, and whose history, of many ruptures during his first year of life, is coming from the Other. The psychoanalyst becomes a reader of what the subject says in a hesitant discourse that finds an ally in the child's play.

What follows will lead us to Lacan's early teachings, or more precisely, to his return to Freud. Lacan takes a road that does not follow subsequent stages. Understanding the subject as a concept is as complex as the clinical practice that lies in the emergence of the unconscious. The history of psychoanalysis with children follows along these lines.

Psychoanalytical listening aims at the subject and his subjective time, not at the person or at an age. To better understand Lacan, we will go over the works of the most relevant psychoanalysts in the field of child psychoanalysis.

Anna Freud

What matters the most to Anna Freud is the internal world and its influence on the external world. She takes what happens on the outside as a force that moves the inside. In this way, she finds a clear difference between 'internal' and 'external' which directly influenced her clinical perspective: "[. . .] the child patient may see 'getting well' in the unpleasurable terms of having to adapt to an unpalatable reality and to give up immediate wish fulfillments. . . . The child's unfinished personality is in a fluid state" (Freud, 1989, p. 106).

To Anna Freud children cannot choose whether or not to start psychoanalysis. Her writings reflect an interesting understanding of 'immaturity' and the absence of choice in that stage of life. It is then expected that complete maturity will be achieved at some point in time, and then the person 'will fall' from the tree. She also refers to a possible paradox in the treatment of children when compared to that of adults. An adult can remember his or her first object relations, while the child does not have the will to leave such relations in an attempt to embrace reality. It is frustrating to the little one not to have anything to remember because of being a child.

In addition, Anna Freud went over the developmental stages that her father proposed (oral, anal, phallic, latency and genital stages) to indicate the stage of the child, clearly showing a sort of order that evidenced the developmental status of the child and the reason why he or she should go through some of the twists and turns of life before reaching a self-sufficient phase; that is, adolescence. This perspective also implies the possibility of making a prognosis (diagnosis) of the child. She writes: "There are many other examples of developmental lines, such as the two given below, where every step is known to the analyst and that can be traced without difficulty, either through working backward by reconstruction from the adult's picture, or through working forward by means of longitudinal analytic exploration and observation of the child" (Freud, 1989, p. 69).

When reading this reference, one can clearly find a clinical proposal that follows certain parameters, either forward or backward, and that uses interpretation as its tool. Anna Freud presents a diagnostic route (*dia* comes from the Greek "through") to point the path by following bidirectional roads. These roads reflect what is expected in each stage of development. In her book, *Normality and Pathology in Childhood*, it is possible to find a table titled "Draft of Diagnostic Profile" in which Anna Freud lists the areas that a clinical history must include to assess a child's development; as a result, one can read: "Child analysis is able to prevent this and, by mitigating the conflicts, to act not only as a therapeutic but as a preventive measure in the truest sense" (Freud, 1989, p. 248).

The preventive character of Anna Freud's child psychoanalysis becomes clear when it involves a possibly perverse or psychotic subject whose psyche could be directed since childhood to avoid any future anomalies. It shows a preventive psychoanalytical approach that aims for normality in adulthood. The treatment is equally important for both parents and child. From this point of view, parents can libidinize the developmental lines where the child has been stranded in order to unblock the libido. What stands out in this sequenced approach to child development is that nowhere do we find Freud's pivotal discoveries, i.e. retroactivity (*nachträglich*) and psychical reality.

Clearly, there are plenty of other thoughts proposed by Anna Freud. Nevertheless, I only mention a few, since it is not the objective of this chapter to thoroughly explore them. My purpose is to locate the place of the child. From Anna Freud's perspective, the infant can be seen as an element that avoids further pathology by means of preventive psychoanalysis. Her psychoanalytical approach leads us to work with a chart of equivalences that refer to what is and what is not normal at a certain age. One can find where the libido has been stranded and the ways to unblock it.

To what extent does the proposal of a developmental line and the means to redirect that stranded libido through psychoanalytical therapy halt the possibility of starting a course of treatment that takes the subject's desire as its core, regardless of age? If it were possible to take psychoanalysis as a preventive measure, wouldn't that make it part of a pedagogy? Does providing the ego of the child with elements that aid in coping with the environment not make a child become obedient? I know that with every question raised here, there are many others that open new ones; however, for the purpose of this work, we will not follow these to the end. The interest is to articulate such questions within the same weave, and to show how Lacan would rethink this theory.

The fact, not less relevant, that mostly women work with children implies that this might be a more suitable task for this gender. Freud predicted that child psychoanalysis would be a field exclusively for women. Only a few male psychoanalysts have adventured their work with children. Among these, we find Donald Winnicott, whose thought has largely contributed to a better understanding of child development, mainly in terms of emotions and culture.

Donald Winnicott

Winnicott makes a unique proposal that joins concepts such as 'holding' and 'handling', 'good-enough mother', 'the false self', 'fear of breakdown', the 'use' of the psychoanalyst, hate in countertransference, a play theory, and probably his most known concepts, 'the transitional object' and 'transitional space'. Lacan would take the all these concepts and theorize the *objet petit a*, which was influenced by Winnicott but is not linked conceptually to the transitional object.

Since play involves anxiety and attempts to elaborate traumatic situations, Winnicott correlates the importance of play with that of free association in the adult analysand. It is Winnicott who while distancing from his teacher, Melanie Klein, and the IPA's principles, created another methodology with children, one that considers treatment even a few months after birth. Both his clinical practice and theory about transitional space came from this conceptual movement, which paradoxically, does not aim to be solved. Transitional play has an effect on the unconscious dynamic. The child builds a transitional space from a non-topological one.

Is it important to mention the characteristics of Winnicott's transitional space; in other words, the paradoxical place where the child locates the transitional objects used in the game that allows a bridge to be built between the 'outside' and the 'inside'. For Winnicott:

- The child assumes rights over the object.
- The object is affectionately cuddled, as well as excitedly loved and mutilated.
- It must never change.
- It must survive instinctual loving, and also hating, and if it be a feature, pure aggressiveness.
- It must seem to the infant to give warmth, or to move, or to have texture, or to do something that seems to show vitality or reality of its own.
- It comes from without (according to the adult's point of view), but not so from the point of view of the baby. Neither does it come from within, it is not a hallucination.
- Its fate is to be gradually decathected, so that in the course of years it becomes not so much forgotten as relegated to limbo. By this I mean that in health the transitional object does not 'go inside' nor does the feeling about it necessarily undergo repression [. . .]. It loses meaning. (Winnicott, 1971, p. 4)

This reference is important because the transitional space concept opens the possibility of a clinical dimension with children from a structural perspective. This perspective differs from Anna Freud's 'insight' (showing the child what is unknown about his or her own unconscious), and from her approach to the external-internal dualism which conveys 'impasses'.

Winnicott's research does not focus on the object as such, but on the first possession, as well as on the intermediate zone between subjectivity and what the child perceives objectively. Winnicott named this first possession "not-me". This is the first reference to differentiation and separation from the primordial object. The teddy-bear does not represent the object-mother, rather the object substitutes the mother's absence while the child is being constituted as a separate entity from the object-mother. He separates by means of an object in his possession that is not a part of himself but that belongs to him.

He also pays special attention to the concept of 'normality', more evident in Anna Freud, which tends to educate the subject. When following Winnicott one cannot think of normality without subjectivity, and so it complicates any attempt to universalize subjective positions and it separates corporal measures from the symbolic building, which results in the symbolic exclusion from corporality. I will even venture to say that the first is cut across by the second, by the symbolic order. Lacan will radically develop his theory from this position.

Returning to Winnicott's thought about 'suspended normality', he says:

> Although from the purely physical standpoint any deviation from health may be taken to be abnormal, it does not follow that physical lowering of health due to emotional strain and stress is necessarily abnormal. This rather startling point of view requires elucidation. . . . A doctor who does not understand the process underlying such unwellness will think out a diagnosis and treat the illness as determined by physical causes.
>
> (Winnicott, 2001, p. 309)

Including the subject's history impacts the way we "read" a clinical session with a child or even with an adult. Winnicott takes Freud's conception of psychic reality, which holds sufficient weight, so that we should reconsider the problem apart from closed discussions that focus on correct development and normality from a biological model.

It is also interesting to think about the tie that exists in children, according to Winnicott, between fantasy and anxiety. The importance of fantasies cannot be underestimated since they hold some sort of truth in themselves. Moving ahead onto a topic I will discuss in more detail, I can now state that fantasies are the material from which symptoms are made. This is why Freud initially got positive therapeutic results, since his patients would tell what they remembered that had happened.

We must not only read childhood experiences literally, because repression and forgotten fragments mix with fantasies in the retelling of a past story. In other words, fantasies cut through the past. So, fantasies are not stories without consequences; rather, they are the discourse that labels the way in which the subject reveals himself and the way his story relates to others and to his own history.

Winnicott uses 'trauma' and its relation with anxiety to exemplify the importance of fantasies.[2] Consequently, a life experience cannot produce significant effects if a subject has not (unconsciously) fantasized about that event, or if there has not been a traumatic experience linked to a representation, or if a meaningful representation from experience has not been built. Such thinking confirms that it is impossible to explain a child's behavior without taking into account his fantasies. In his 1926 work *Inhibitions, Symptoms and Anxiety* (Freud, 1925/2016), Freud would point out that in order for the outside world experiences to resonate within the child they must be tied to the ego through a prior to interiorization.

In relation to the notion of a prior mental structure that (Winnicott, 2001) developed in 1936 in "Appetite and Emotional Disorder", he states that children, including newborn babies, possess a complex mental structure. From this point of view, we have a child that somehow has a certain psychical structure since birth, which makes itself evident in the way the baby establishes a bond with the mother or the caregiver, always by means of food.

At the beginning, the child is not only fed food but also the representation of food. This is what Winnicott thinks about the existence of a complex structure, a problem that Freud raises in *Project for a Scientific Psychology* when he mentions that hallucination is an attempt to ease the pain, and that it offers a long-lasting decrease of displeasure.

Another important observation about the newborn child has to do with the assertion (somehow scandalous) "that there is nothing that can be named a baby" (Winnicott, 2001, p. 138), at the same time, it does not deny the existence of the potential product. This seems interesting because on one hand, it is known that there is a complex mental structure in the newborn, and, on the other, even when he cannot be named 'baby', he is granted a status of being an individual. To Winnicott, individuation is anticipated by what is known as "organization of collective individuation" (Winnicott, 2001, p. 138) placing the newborn humanization in a whole organization. Winnicott does not consider that the newborn is capable of body coordination, even when he has a mental structure. In exchange, the newborn suffers anxieties that are part of a paranoid position (following Klein) and what neutralizes these anxiety states is childhood care. About this, Freud says:

> Here a removal of the stimulus can only be effected by an intervention which will temporarily stop the release of quantity [. . .] in the interior of the body, and an intervention of this kind requires an alteration in the external world (e.g., the supply of nourishment or the proximity of the sexual object), and this, as a 'specific action', can only be brought about in particular ways. At early stages the human organism is incapable of

achieving this specific action. It is brought about by extraneous help, when the attention of an experienced person has been drawn to the child's condition by a discharge taking place along the path of internal change (e.g., by the child's screaming). This path of discharge thus acquires an extremely important secondary function of bringing about an *understanding* with other people; and the original helplessness of human beings is thus the *primal source* of all *moral motives*.

(Freud, 1895/1953, p. 379)

This reference is fundamental, not only because of its scope of morality, but also because of its acuteness to stress the role of the person who relieves displeasure. As has been said, such an action not only feeds, but also nourishes the fragmented body with symbolism. At first, evidently, the infant does not own his own body and that is why he requires that someone else bring about the specific action. Winnicott considers this to be a pivotal point in the individuation process, a process that is carried by another person.

Unlike Freud and Lacan, Winnicott envisions a kind of anxiety in the newborn child that will play a unifying role (acting as a limit) in future moments in life. The absence of anxiety does not avoid regression. In other words, anxiety, according to Winnicott, acts as a deterrent to regression during the first childcare experiences which unify and individuate the future child. Fear does not appear before danger, but before the absence of anxiety, which sets a limit to the individual.

According to Winnicott, the child's early adaptation to the environment is key to develop "adequate mental health". In the best of cases, the child goes through the discovery of the environment without losing his sense of being (to Winnicott the being is within the organization of collective-individuation; it is not an isolated unit of the environment). The mother, through her care and nourishment, supplies the child with the tools required to adequately adapt to the environment.

The result of a poor adaptation to the environment has as consequence, "a psychotic distortion in the organization of collective-individuation" (Winnicott, 2001, p. 300). This premise is based on the primitive emotional developmental phases, which hold similarity to the observed phenomena in adult schizophrenia. As it has been mentioned, we must add the role of illusion whose function is to be in between the environment and the individual.

Furthermore, if what potentially creates an individual derives from necessity, and prepares hallucination, it also allows the child to use illusion as a space between what surrounds him and himself. Now, if we think of that illusion as the thumb the child sucks when being away from the breast, or as part of the blanket that he plays with the most, we then understand that illusion creates a paradoxical space; in other words, a transitional space.

Therefore, anxiety plays a role in the future constitution of the individual (as so does the mother and her care), and it aims to unify the child who was originally fragmented. Even as a fragmented "child", he possesses a complex psychical structure that allows him, out of need, to make of hallucination a way to satisfy these needs. However, the baby needs someone else's help, because, as we know, he is completely helpless at birth.

Winnicott's main contribution to psychoanalysis is the transitional object. The transitional object works as an illusion that mediates between the individual and his surroundings. It is a paradoxical place that does not need to be or should not be solved. The transitional object is: "not a comforter, but a soother. It was a sedative that always worked. This is a typical example of what I'm calling a *transitional object* [. . .]. When Y was a little boy it was always certain that if anyone gave him his 'Baa' he would immediately suck it and lose anxiety" (Winnicott, 2001, p. 315). Then he adds that the transitional objects and phenomena belong to the realm of illusion which is at the base of experience. This early stage of development is possible thanks to the special capacity that the mother has to adapt to the child's needs, allowing the illusion that the things he creates actually exist (Winnicott, 2001, p. 324).

Childhood anxiety (related to disintegration) and the transitional object as a sedative are then knotted together. What matters is not the symbolic value of the mother as a representative, but the actual object that the child has, and this primary possession works as something that differs from the child: a 'not-me'. The relevance of this notion is that the actual object is more important than what it symbolizes, for example, the breast. This approach, and his notion of object relations, is what separates Winnicott's thinking from Klein's internal object and object relations.

Finally, we know about the influence that the English psychoanalyst had on Melanie Klein, an influence that he acknowledged; however, she would go on to develop her own line of thought.

Melanie Klein

According to Élisabeth Roudinesco's and Michel Plon's *Dictionary of Psychoanalysis*: "Kleinism is not just a movement, but a school comparable with Lacanism. It has been constituted as a system of thought" (Roudinesco and Plon, 1998, p. 598).

The Kleinian revolution is a reformulation of a number of Freud's theoretical ideas. One of these is to integrate, as part of treatment, psychotic patient cases in the work with children. Klein did not intend to build a type of pedagogy based on psychoanalytical principles that provided 'correct' forms of child development.

Klein also conducted research on the Oedipus complex. For her, it is the mother, and not the father, who has a primordial relationship with the child. An element to consider is that when theorizing these 'positions', she believes that madness is in the heart of the human being, as part of his structure; this proposal would lead Lacan to link his psychiatric practice with psychoanalysis.

Among the most relevant elements that differentiate Klein from Lacan is the lack of a thorough epistemological foundational study, being one of these the notion of the *nachträglich*, so fundamental to Freud and Lacan's work. Neither does Klein put forward a subjective dimension, which is central to Lacan's theory. We will return to these concepts as we advance forward.

The image that almost automatically comes to our minds when we think of Klein is that of child psychoanalysis. Although she made great contributions to psychoanalytical practice on adults, for our purposes here, we will focus on her work with children. It is interesting to note that Klein differs almost completely from Anna Freud. Klein proposes that a child must be in a psychoanalytical treatment as part of education. To analyze the child, it is not necessary that the presence of symptoms disturb him or his parents:

> We shall let the child acquire as much sexual information as the growth of its desire for knowledge requires, thus depriving sexuality at once of its mystery and of great part of its danger. This ensures that wishes, thoughts and feelings shall not – as happened to us – be partly repressed and partly, in so far repression fails, endured under a burden of false shame and nervous suffering. In averting this repression, this burden of superfluous suffering, moreover, we are laying the foundations for health, mental balance and the favorable development of character.
>
> (Klein, 1990, p. 16)

This is how Klein introduces herself as the one responsible for the child's treatment. Another characteristic of Klein's technical approach is that parents are not part of the treatment. Interventions are based on direct interpretations to the patient, a practice that has been severely criticized.

When thinking about the aim of Klein's psychoanalytical interpretations, we have to take anxiety as the thread to follow, because as we have and continue to see, anxiety plays a critical role in clinical practice. It is not coincidental that both Winnicott and Klein took this concept as a pivotal part of their theoretical building.

According to Klein, anxiety can be observed very early in life. It appears in the form of a threat of dismemberment, fragmentation and persecution against which the infant has to defend. In these same lines, Klein considers that object relations are present from the earliest stages of life; these are partial, not whole. The newborn splits the object (maternal breast), an object that will either satisfy or frustrate and that will lead to love-hate relations, which support 'introjection' and 'projection' mechanisms. What is experienced as 'good' is introjected, while the 'bad' is projected; hence, the notion of 'good-breast' and 'bad-breast'. It is evident that this concept does not refer to a physical part of the body, but to the mental representation that the child creates from the object.

A bad object is 'attacked' through the child's unconscious phantasies about that object. The objective of putting into effect such defenses is to protect the unintegrated ego. This differs from the Freudian ego theory in the sense that there is no ego as such. However, Klein's proposal coincides with Winnicott's; they both think there is an ego, but it remains disintegrated, and it is the mother who turns the split ego into a unified self.

About the emergence of anxiety in the newborn, Klein says that it is an effect of the death instinct within the organism, which is experienced as fear of annihilation (death) and that is introduced as fear of persecution.

What matters, then, is to acknowledge that these movements are caused by phantasy. In such movements, the child splits the object as well as the ego to protect himself or herself from anxiety. Klein considers projective identification to be another defense mechanism, which produces an aggressive relationship with the object. In other words, projective identification comes from the drive to damage the object (mother), while attempting to control it. A 'normal' development is based on the equilibrium between the mechanism of introjection and projection that the infant achieves.

As we can see, phantasy is the field upon which interpretation and theorization are founded. This raises the following question: what is phantasy to Melanie Klein? According to Harari: "Phantasy strictly means, as specified by Susan Isaacs: an unconscious mental content that can or cannot become conscious" (Harari, 1990, p. 18).

This reference reveals that phantasy is the mental expression of instincts. Indeed, the language that Klein uses has a biological tone. For example, she speaks of instincts, while the German word Freud uses is *Trieb* (a drive or an urge). These slight differences in nuance lead to confusion and often cause difficulties.

Going back to the concept of phantasy, we should not think of it as an escape from "reality" in its most literal sense. Phantasy is closer to the life experiences and events which the infant or newborn undergoes. It can even be said that phantasy influences the way someone responds to experience. As Winnicott proposes, if some part of the world (environment) causes effects on the child, it is because the world has been linked to phantasy. In other words, phantasy affects the way a child perceives and acts within his or her own context.

Phantasy also works as a defense mechanism from internal reality. Freud considered that the role of hallucination is to decrease the displeasure that the needs (hunger, sexual impulse) produce. In a similar way, phantasies according to Klein achieve the same goal and more, since they refer not only to an external reality, but also to an internal one. It is not merely about the organic displeasure that hunger causes; it is about its representation as part of an internal reality.

What we can think from Klein's work is that unconscious phantasies determine personality, both within the self and internal objects (Segal, 2006). Therefore, a great part of her interventions, in both adults and children, are about the patient's phantasies. Consequently, the objective is to make sense ('here and now') of what the patient recovers from his past, always taking into account (to valuate) the presence of the psychoanalyst.

In Kleinian analysis, the function of the psychoanalyst plays a constitutive role. In other words, the mother is radically important because she is the one who will ensure that the persecutory phantasies of the child do not predominate and that the integration of a stronger self is achieved. In the same way, the psychoanalyst must value this role and move the patient from a schizo-paranoid position to a depressive one. This concept is clinically and theoretically fundamental since interpretations aim to integrate a self out of a fragmented beginning. Klien states that with the introduction of the object during the first year of the infant, an integration process occurs. The love and hate that the infant experienced as separate from his mother are now brought together. Such synthesis results in an increasing fear of loss, a strong sentiment of guilt and states that resemble mourning. These feelings appear as a consequence of experiencing aggressive impulses toward the loved object. According to Klein, here is where depression emerges (Klein, 1990).

It is important to note that this movement carries a certain amount of envy, which lies in the notion that the child does not only project the bad within the object, but also the good. The mother, therefore, must act as a mediator, because in some extreme cases the ego projects all the good within the object and keeps the bad (in phantasy), avoiding, in this way, the integration of personality.

The work of the Kleinian psychoanalyst holds similarities to what the mother would do, that is, to unify objects, to go from having partial objects to integrating whole objects. This is why interpretation is needed for clarification. Interpretation aims at making sense of what the child brings to consultation. The patient brings certain material that he does not seem to understand, and then the psychoanalyst returns this material to the patient with an interpretation that unifies the split object and integrates it. In such a way, Kleinian analysis seeks to re-introject the good that has been projected, while the psychoanalyst mediates this work. About this, Harari thinks: "Klienians fall into the consistent misconception of making their analysands believe that every-thing that happens to them is because by means of their phantasies, they want it that way. Thus, they unceasingly work with interventions directed towards the ego without recognizing these as such" (Harari, 1990, p. 28).

Nevertheless, not all psychoanalysts that work with children agree with this position. Such is the case of French psychoanalyst Françoise Dolto.

Françoise Dolto

Unlike Anna Freud, Klein and Winnicott, Dolto not only was Lacan's con-temporary, she was also his great friend. Her theories are fundamentally sup-ported through clinical practice wherein the psychoanalyst in each case works from a not-knowing position.

Dolto's point of view about clinical work with children is certainly influ-enced by her relationship with Lacan. She takes some of Lacan's concepts to build her own work. This adaptation did not only relate to language but to technique, and to a new approach, one that used the language of the child. With small children, she recommends not using tests or seeking a clarifying interpretation. It is important to mention that she allowed an active participa-tion from other psychoanalysts while she was with her child-patient, which resulted in an extremely interesting approach. She asserted that there are no child-analysts but only psychoanalysts who work with children. In this sense, her proposal is somehow related with Lacan's theories on the subject.

Furthermore, Dolto used the word 'subject' to designate the person who is being analyzed regardless of his age. It is worth mentioning that this notion will have important repercussions throughout this book. Dolto's position also emphasizes listening and how language is used with the child. She does not turn to highly elaborated interpretations; on the contrary, she uses her patient's own language as a way of listening without adding external signi-fiers to the child's speech.

In 1977, Dolto would say:

> If psychoanalysis with children makes sense, it is only because it allows the analysis of the repressed; that is, of that time that preceded the child's current life. If our interpretations refer to the child's present relationships, then it is not psychoanalysis but a supportive therapy. What makes it psy-choanalysis is that all of what is ongoing between the child and the people in his life does not concern us. This is the psychoanalyst's own castration.
> (Dolto, 1977)

What we can interpret from this statement is that Dolto believes it is fun-damental for the psychoanalyst who works with children to listen and to be aware of the 'unconscious image of the body'. To propose the premise of the 'unconscious image of the body', Dolto refers to autism as a means to analysis, for example, in the case of Dominique. According to her, autism is the result of a break in the mother-child bond. Such fracture is contrary to the one in psychosis where the image of the body is somehow preserved. This is not the same image as the one in Lacan's 'Mirror Stage', nor is it the image in Klein's and Winnicott's theory of a fragmented body. This is Dolto's own contribution.

The fracture in the mother-child bond does not refer to the mother's real body, but to what Dolto calls a 'symboligenous bond', the unconscious image of the body. The child can lose this bond without the mother being actually absent. When the child is abandoned, he will try to replace the lost bond, the lost object, with a part of his body. The way he defends himself against annihilation anxiety is by means of hallucination as a primitive source of satisfaction. In this way, when the infant seeks satisfaction through hallucination, he distances himself from the symbolic interchange with the mother.

Dolto is the first psychoanalyst to introduce psychosis as the product of three generations. For her, autism is tied to desire and the law. In this sense, there is something in the core of a subject that cannot be symbolized. The subject has not been redirected by means of castration: "Dolto distances herself from Lacan. For Lacan the signifier Name-of-the-Father is missing in the symbolic weave itself. For Dolto, what psychosis is missing is a certain experience. Its 'actualization' in analysis and its 're-inscription' in language will lead to a new relationship with the symbolic order" (Yannick, 1990, p. 136).

This proposal tends to reincorporate the motherly experience that was not received and to return it as a symbol that would tie a knot, correcting in this way, what had failed to be constructed. Lacan will reconsider this as the 'foreclosure' of the signifier. From his standpoint there are no means to reincorporate the signifier within the logic of the symbolic chain. The rupture with what is symbolic (with the presence of the mother) results in the hallucinated presence of the maternal body through the child's own corporal sensations. Therefore, even though the psychotic child is not completely excluded from the symbolic realm, it is impossible for him to access the symbolic code.

Before Dolto, this issue had not been approached in terms of the body. Fantasies, instincts, self-cohesion, ego-pedagogy had been part of the psychoanalytical discussion, but it was Dolto who, for the first time stated that the body represents each subject. She introduced the subject in child psychoanalysis and Lacan would extend it in his theory. Dolto asserts that the body is the instrument that the child has to bond with others, the environment and his mother.

> The body image belongs to each subject. It is linked to the subject and his history. It is specific in each under a given situation and a libidinous

relation. It is fundamentally unconscious and can become partly precon-
scious if it is associated to conscious language, which uses metaphors,
and metonymies that refer to the body image in terms of mimes based on
the structure of language, as well as on spoken language.

(Yannick, 1990, p. 137)

Body image is the living synthesis of our emotional experiences: inter-
human, repetitively experienced through elective erogenous sensations,
archaic or current. It is the symbolic unconscious incarnation of the desiring subject that has existed since conception.

(Dolto, 1984, p. 21)

Dolto's proposal, therefore, is to listen to what the child says through his
words, gestures or playing.

Playing exists not to amuse, but as a form of language where the signifier
appears for the psychoanalyst to read. This provides the child with tools
that with time will allow understanding the origin of his or her suffering.

(Dolto, 1984, pp. 24–25)

Parting from this notion, we can now say that theory cannot be separated
from technique, since both are an equal part of child analysis. What makes a
difference are the resources called upon for each. The child's unconscious is
revealed by symptoms, dreams and fantasies that will take a main role in the
psychoanalytical process. The symbolic value, and to a great extent, unconscious, of the ludic and graphic material enables the analyst to approach the
child's set of problems and to intervene by providing the missing words to
the child's discourse. The psychoanalyst needs to be careful enough to use
the patient's signifiers without asking the child what his words mean to him.

In analysis, this does not disturb development nor prevent the appearance of
neurosis. The psychoanalytical work is not prophylactic, educational or aimed
to heal. It is about accompanying the child and favoring understandings about
the events he or she is undergoing. Psychoanalysis differs from psychotherapies in both practice and theory. Generally, psychotherapies seek to re-educate
or to re-adapt. What matters in psychoanalysis is to reveal an un-whole truth
within each subject, to learn about the direction of his or her own desire. It
seeks a subjective change that would allow the subject to have a view of the
events that happened in his life from different perspectives.

In *Psychoanalysis for Children* (Fendrik, 1989), Argentinian psychoanalyst
Silvia Fendrick reflected on the theoretical and clinical differences between
Anna Freud and Melanie Klein. The first tended to prophylaxis; therefore,
she could not accurately separate her theory from pedagogy. Klein favored

transference as the element that would determine the beginning of the child's psychoanalytical treatment. They both used playing techniques; however, their approach to it was widely different.

Finally, Dolto's methodological proposal had great repercussions in the recent landscape of psychoanalysis with children. By conversing with the child, Dolto was able to provoke a spontaneous speech. Her main ideas are presented in her book *Psychoanalysis and Pediatrics* (Dolto, 1991) in which she includes a number of cases taken from her clinical experience from her work with child patients over many years. In this book, she also stresses how important it is for the child to pay for his own session. The child pays with an object that he creates himself; in other words, a symbolic payment.

A Lacanian perspective for child psychoanalysis

We have already discussed some of the theories referring to child psychoanalysis. With the exception of Dolto, the theorists mentioned in this chapter think of the child from an empirical perspective and not in terms of the role that he or she plays in the family. The child occupies a place in the parents' psychical reality. This point of view does not deny the empirical dimension of the child, or how the parents bring the child to the psychoanalyst's office and what happens while they are waiting outside. The main difference is how the psychoanalyst listens to the desire or to the demand of the child. The psychoanalyst reads the signifiers that the child carries as a constituent part of his or her own subjectivity.

This perspective presents difficulties because it implies that what matters beyond the child as a 'person' is in reality the child as an 'event'. Not only does the child occupy a place in his or her parents' ideal, but the child also transgresses and halts their history.

To better understand this idea, we must refer to Lacan's teaching and the emphasis he places on the signifier and retroactivity, as well as the death drive and its link to language or *lalangue*. All of these, except for *lalangue*, are Freudian concepts reformulated by Lacan and they radically differ from his contemporaries' work.

To say that something is 'Lacanian' goes beyond using this adjective in an effort to show that one theory is better than another. Psychoanalysts use this 'Lacanian' perspective as a reading tool in their clinical practice. Before we move forward, it is important to remember Lacan's phrase from his seminar in Caracas: "It is up to you to be Lacanian if you wish; I am Freudian". It is certainly impossible to think of Freudian psychoanalysis without thinking of Lacan after being captivated by his perspective. Freud was a seed, which Lacan nurtured to fruition, not without consequence.

On this matter, Lacan built most of his teachings and thought via his seminars. In this sense, there was one concept Lacan considered to be his sole invention: the *objet petit a*. Furthermore, he took Heidegger's rigor to reveal the Freudian unconscious. He was also fascinated by Frege's mathematical theories, which he borrowed to take psychoanalysis to the realm of logics. He would also use topology to reconsider the place the subject has within the theory of the unconscious.

After developing 'the subject of the unconscious' theory, Lacan used it as an argument against ego-strengthening treatments that favored a therapeutic approach, and not a structural one. Lacan would say in 1949: "[The child psychoanalyst] is being constantly required to invent technical and instrumental resources that turn control analysis sessions and study groups of child psychoanalysis into a moveable frontier for psychoanalytical conquest" (Miller, 1987, p. 22).

In such matter, a new type of clinical practice had been introduced. One which is not sustained on anecdotal dialogues with patients, nor on medical observations; neither is it directed through 'the imaginary'. It is a practice that takes what the patient says to produce 'misunderstandings'.

Consequently, a child psychoanalytical practice based on Lacan refers to a particular intervention and to a way of thinking each case, for example, taking into account the school's demands, the parent's transference, and what the child says that may or may not be different from the adult's position.

From a Lacanian perspective, it is possible to consider a treatment in child analysis that takes the child between the coordinates of desire, as are phantasy, drive and the lack of the signifier in the Other; coordinates that occupy the upper level of the graph of desire. These fall into a logic formulation of the subject based on Lacan's thoughts about masculine or feminine subjective position toward desire and *jouissance*.

In relation to the child, desire transgresses the limit of time and invests in the reality of the future, generating an illusion for both the girl and the boy. The challenge in psychoanalysis is to allow the emergence of such an illusion ('phantasmatic') that organizes desire in the boy or girl. This imaginary dot where the child condenses his entire narcissistic ideal is the structuring mark of subjective positions, which find its energy in repression and in the resolution of the Oedipus complex. In other words, the child-subject ignores that the symbolic order is an important part in this imaginary projection.

The fact that the child learns to speak of his or her own figurative and imaginary projections raises the question about the equivalence that exists between figuration and discourse, and leaves the question unanswered. For Lacanian psychoanalysis, the capture of the subject by the signifier (symbolic order) already operates in figuration (imaginary order). For the child, nevertheless, the drawing or the act of playing (the real) is effective precisely because it involves real objects. This crucial idea, central to my work, will unfold throughout the following chapters.

I can venture to say that Lacan's clinical 'radicalism' lies in his introduction of the *objet petit a*. If desire is central to Freud's work, it is Lacan who formalizes this premise. Lacan drifts from a clinical stage to a clinical writing; what he achieves is a type of listening that builds a link with the child-analysand. The *objet petit a* – defined as remainder, surplus *jouissance*, indomitable, impossible, incalculable – is that heterogeneous element of writing that through its inherent impossibility provides possibility, therefore reaching formality in the theory of discourse. Even though the unconscious is structured as a language, it is not language. There is always a return of the repressed and unconscious formations that exceed the order of language. Language aims at the unconscious but it is not the unconscious itself.

If we read Freud thoroughly, we notice that desire is pivotal in his practice. Libido is the energy that moves desire and such desire is always sexual. The etymological root for libido evokes a lack; it is a desire, a lack or a wish. For Lacan, the *objet petit a* is what represents the absence of an object that satisfies a drive. It also operates the lack and the enigma of the absence of object; however, it does not seek to solve or name this lack.

The *objet petit a*, as both lack and surplus-enjoyment, elicits the question that rises in our practice with the child-analysand. Lacan maintains that "the child is the only *objet petit a*" (Lacan, 1955). Although this is certainly a clear statement, the aim of this book is to expand upon this assertion and to reflect on whether or not the child is, in fact, more than an *objet petit a*.

Finally, to close this chapter, it is worthwhile to quote Agamben in order to set down the roads we will be exploring throughout the book. He says:

> [. . .] the infancy at issue here, cannot merely be something which chronologically precedes language and which, at a certain point, ceases to exist in order to spill into speech. It is not a paradise which, at a certain moment, we leave forever in order to speak; rather, it coexists in its origins with language – indeed, its itself constituted through the appropriation of it by language in each instance to produce the individual as a subject.
>
> (Agamben, 1993, p. 48)

For Agamben, infancy takes the subject – yet to become – to a pre-linguistic, mute domain that lacks words or experience. Infancy abandons an ineffable world to enter a mystical realm; this passage is what allows the emergence of experience. What this passage demands is that infancy falls and that it is captured by language, an event that originates language and makes it impossible for mute experience to become, simultaneously, a subjective experience.

Infancy as 'psychical substance' is a pre-subjective operation similar to a pre-linguistic subject.

Such an understanding is important because for Lacan, there is no pre-linguistic subject. Agamben opens a possibility to consider the existence of a subjectivity separated from the use of power or discourse since, according to Foucault, any subject is a product of knowledge/power. How do we name a pre-linguistic subject? *Infancy*.

For Agamben, Freud and Lacan, infancy occurs in a possible relationship between the subject and language. The difference is that Agamben questions historical linearity, and considers the existence of a pre-subjective infancy, that which precedes language. For Freud, sexuality plays a predominant role in infancy that is carried throughout the history of every subject. If infancy is organized in the framework of desire, then the drive for the child becomes of the utmost importance and consequently the concept of sexuality is extended. For Lacan, the subject takes place within structure. The subject, therefore, is structured and delimited in relation with the language phenomena. In this matter, the child, or even infancy, is confined to a symbolic universe that allows the subject to recognize himself *in* and *with* the Other. Thus, Lacan introduces the term *infans* to refer to the time in which the *child-subject* does not yet speak.

Infancy then characterizes the fundamental nature of language for human beings and opens a space for history; it is a product of a subjective operation. Every time the *child* speaks, he cuts through and renews history, making of it an interval, a discontinuity, an *epokhé*, or a historization rather than a linear movement. From Agamben's understanding of 'infancy' and Lacan's perspective of 'the child', we can conclude these concepts are signifiers that will always lack signification.

Notes

1 In psychoanalysis, the issue of responsibility has led to a wide discussion among psychoanalysts who work with "the child" and those who receive a child but aim their listening to the subject and the network of relations that engulf him or her. This is still a controversial field. It is well known that Lacan has revisited this idea and places the subject in the foreground, not the child (person or individual). What matters, therefore, is a responsibility based on subjective (unconscious) and not on legal (conscious) premises. At the same time, this raises the question about how the child is involved in language when he or she is introduced into the clinical experience.

2 In his work, the most primitive anxiety is associated with unsafe support. The lack of kind nourishment can result in a disintegrated, de-personalized feeling and also in the crystallization of a false *self*. Anxiety is normal when there are failures in the child's care. Nonetheless, Winnicott underlines that the lack of anxiety is a sign of a regressive state of no return. He agrees with Freud's notion that anxiety is a symbol of separation and states that an individual must have a certain degree of ability and maturity to express what he or she feels. Therefore, a baby could hardly experience anxiety at birth. In this

way he sets aside the conception that birth trauma determines an anxiety pattern. Winnicott considers that in some cases birth trauma determines the pattern of persecution, this is, the way to express anxiety.

Bibliography

Agamben, G. (1993). *Infancy and History*. London: Verso.

Dolto, F. (1977). *Lettre de l'ecole freudienne de Paris*. Paris: Gallimard

Dolto, F. (1984). *La Imagen Inconsciente del Cuerpo*. Buenos Aires: Paidós.

Dolto, F. (1991). *Psicoanálisis y pediatría*. México: Siglo XXI.

Fendrik, S. (1989). *Psicoanálisis para niños*. Buenos Aires: Amorrortu.

Freud, A. (1989). *Normality and Pathology in Childhood: Assessments of Development*. London: Karnac Books.

Freud, S. (1895/1953). *Project for a Scientific Psychology. S. E., 1*. London: Hogarth.

Freud, S. (1925/2016). *Inhibición, síntoma y angustia*. Buenos Aires: Amorrortu editores.

Harari, R. (1990). *Fantasma: Fin de Análisis?* Buenos Aires: Nueva Visión.

Klein, M. (1990). El desarrollo de un niño. *Obras Completas. Amor, Culpa y Reparación, 1*. Buenos Aires: Paidós.

Lacan, J. (1955). *El Seminario de Jacques Lacan 14*. Buenos Aires: GAMA Producción Gráficas SRL.

Miller, J.-A. (1987). *Escisión, Excomunión, Disolución. Tres momentos en la visa de Jacques Lacan*. Buenos Aires: Manantial.

Roudinesco, E. and Plon, M. (1998). *Diccionario de Psicoanálisis*. Barcelona: Paidós.

Segal, H. (2006). *Introducción a la Obra de Melanie Klein*. Barcelona: Paidós.

Winnicott, D. (1971). *Playing and Reality*. London: Tavistock Publications.

Winnicott, D. (2001). *Collected Papers: Through Paediatrics to Psycho-Analysis*. London: Tavistock Publications.

Yannick, F. (1990). *Francoise Dolto: De la Ética a la Práctica del Psicoanalisis en Niños*. Buenos Aires: Nueva Vision.

Chapter 2

The infantile and the child in Freudian theory

*The unspeakable is not indecision. The unspeakable is a coincidence in oppo-
sition . . . it's in this contradiction where the impossibility for a speech with
oneself dwells.*

Part I

What do we understand as "the infantile" in Freudian theory? What is a child
in psychoanalysis? What is the infantile?[1] The child? These are questions that
could be answered loosely, by locating the issues that are part of a certain
moment of an individual's life; for example, a child is that who is younger
than ten years old. This way, we would prevent many complications, even
though the problem is that the infantile cannot be reduced to this posture.

When starting to talk, the child as subject does nothing more than shatter
himself or herself (in) language, as Joyce did. The gap in the infantile appears
in the subject's saying. Borges writes: "Time is the substance I am made of.
Time is a river which sweeps me along, but I am the river; it is a tiger which
destroys me, but I am the tiger; it is a fire which consumes me, but I am the
fire. The world, unfortunately, is real; I, unfortunately, am Borges" (Borges,
1980, p. 301).

The whirlpool in which we are submerged since we are children can be
read. It can also be read that the time is referenced in language, being "the
time [. . .] The substance [that] I am made of". That is how Freud found that
"the unimportant" contains the core of the being, which does not indicate an
origin but a beginning.

In the beginning was the pain that pushes to life, inscription of absence that
moves that which is lost since always. Every birth keeps in its memory a trace,
a mark of pain. Freud points: "Any psychological theory deserving consideration must provide an explanation of memory" (Freud, 1950a/1953, p. 343).

In analysis, the analysand talks about his or her history, about the memory
that, being a trace of what is not there anymore, leaves a testimony of what

was and what will never be again. If we gave memory a different name (after the Freud in the *Project*), it would be "lasting traces", the space in which the infantile exercises its influence on the subject's present.

These are the marks that Joyce left unresolved at the end of *A Portrait of the Artist as a Young Man*, in which, as an enigma, he makes a cut to articulate what was said in the family's history: "Old father, old artificer, stand me now and ever in good stead" (Joyce, 2006, p. 240).

Such words indicate that something from history leaves an indelible mark that is reflected in the particularity in each subject, evidently with the erotic charge that every demand has in itself.

But let us go back to Freud. Despite the metaphor-ridden language referring to physics and chemistry in his first works, it is interesting to see his three "registers", which are the economical, the topical and the dynamic. In these registers, by not being physically thought, or separated from each other by being implicated, the structure – once more – becomes evident without it being located in the body. Even as early as "Letter 52", Freud had described a certain functioning of the psychic apparatus where, from the transcriptions and re-transcriptions, memory had a place in a non-corporeal *topos*, thus opening, for the first time, a virtual space in which the subject's location is in Another place, that is, in another scene.

The importance of talking about places that are not located spatially makes it necessary to create, as Freud did in chapter VII of *The Interpretation of Dreams*, figures that allow their representation.

Dreams and the infantile

With dreams we can find a certain aroma of remnant in the plot of the infantile. And by underlining it, psychoanalysis does not centralize it, but if it is integrated into the analysand's speech it fulfills a function. How would it be to give it a role of non-remnant?

To answer, we could imagine Freud insisting on "knowing" the dream that the dreamer had during the night, and the account being a faithful reflection of that oneiric experience; an exact correspondence between the word and the thing. The dream as such is lost, what remains is what the subject articulates in words and silences, stammering, making mistakes and so forth.

Curiously, the only way to make the dream present is to "disfigure" the "dreamed" dream, in an effort to give it some coherence.

> It is true that we distort the dream in our attempt to reproduce it; we once more find therein what we have called the secondary and often misunderstanding elaboration of the dream by the agency of normal

thinking. But this distortion is itself no more than a part of the elaboration to which the dream-thoughts are constantly subjected as a result of the dream-censorship.

(Freud, 1900a/1953)

However, as far as remnant, it takes its dimension from the dreamer's speech for not being able to account for it, because there are no words to name it entirely. Not for being lost does it stop having an effect on the subject. Without a lost dream, there is no account. If the dream could be recovered just as it was dreamed in the oneiric experience, we could call it a "not lost" dream, and there would be no "need" to tell it or, therefore, to interpret it. Language would be adapted to the Thing and the time would just be an organized succession.

Let us go back now to the dream in relation with the infantile. It is possible to think that both the infantile and the "lost" dream have the function of tying the subject's saying, because they are both in the order of the impossible, which makes logical time (*Nachträglich, après coup*) necessary to allow this new clinical display. We can see this with an example, an *indirect* patient of Freud, Little Hans.

When Hans, a five-year-old boy, dreams that he is playing with the girls in his class to "*wee-wee*", the posture that the dream takes is clear as the fulfillment of a desire. The intention of doing *something* – that they make him "*wee-wee*" – is also present, that by being part of the oneiric content it leaves a trace of what could not be accomplished in waking and it somehow moves to the dream as a means of fulfillment, even when once he is awake he asks his father to take him some place where these girls do not see him. Repression lowers its guard in the dream leaving a free range to processing from one representation to another, this way the fragmentation of linear time can be seen. Freud draws the scene thus: " [. . .] *We find the child and the child's impulses still living on in the dream*" (Freud, 1900a/1953, p. 206).

It turns out that the temporal dimension is surpassed by the oneiric experiences, at the same time that it places the infantile as the content's producer in the dream. The experiences in the first infancy combined with daytime experiences shape the adults' dreams. This does not diminish the importance of the actual experiences; however, the infantile becomes stronger inasmuch as it can be read in the oneiric speech, where the common factor is the timelessness of the dissatisfaction of the drive motion, which looks to be repeated over and over.

The link that Freud makes between the infantile and the dream bearing in mind the properties of both is not something that surfaces *ex nihilo* in epistemological terms. What we will quote next allows us to observe what has been mentioned so far more clearly:

> If they [*conscious thoughts*] have forced their way anywhere to our per-
> ception we discover from the analysis of the symptom formed that these
> normal thoughts have been subjected to normal treatment and *have been
> transformed into the symptom by means of condensation and compromise
> formation, through superficial associations, under cover of contradic-
> tions, and eventually over the road of regression.* In view of complete
> identity found between the peculiarities of the dream-work and of the psy-
> chic activity forming the psychoneurotic symptoms, we shall be justified
> in transferring to the dream the conclusions urged upon us by hysteria.
>
> (Freud, 1900a/1953, p. 587)

This bridge laid out from hysteria to the dream is related to what in 1957 Lacan called "the formations of the unconscious".

The news we get through such manifestations have a sexual hint, even though it is veiled. Or, to say it better, what is repressed (moving affection) and later surfaces as a manifestation of the unconscious has its origins in motions of infantile sexual desires. In *The Interpretation of Dreams*, despite the infantile being the agent that pushes the oneiric formation, Freud doubted the possibility of invoking the sexual and the infantile to complement his the-ory of the dream, due to him not having enough clinical material to explore it. Said doubt is returned to in the link between the wit and the dream and the unconscious (Freud, 1905c/1953), where he again ensures the first infancy as the source of the unconscious, being the processes of unconscious through the ones that come completely from it.

The infantile is not only related to the dream and the symptom, but also to wit. Freud says that the unconscious is a form of thought, that's why it is called a formation of the unconscious. Well then, the laughter caused by wit is an infantile feature of thought:

> [. . .] It would seem very tempting to transfer the desired specific char-
> acter of the comic into the awakening of the *infantile*, and to conceive
> the comic as a regaining of "lost infantile laughing". One could then say,
> "I laugh every time over a difference of expenditure between the other
> and myself, when I discover in the other the child". [. . .] This laughter
> would thus result every time from the comparison between the ego of the
> grown-up and the ego of the child.
>
> (Freud, 1905c/1953, pp. 212–213)

Both in wit and oneiric formation, the infantile works as the copperwood of the unconscious, besides avoiding an excessive expense of psychic energy.

Up to this moment we find – in Freud – that *what drives in the unconscious is the infantile emotional life*, which would bring the great complication of marking the difference between the unconscious material that does not concern the infantile properly and the one that does. Following this line, it is worth asking: if the unconscious is where the representations of the repressed infantile life dwell, as well as some others, what is the material these are made of? The question is a complex one, and it seems to find an answer when Freud says: "the unconscious in our psychic life is the infantile" (Freud, 1916–1917a/1953, p. 193).

Smoothing things over, this quote is an equivalence between the infantile and the unconscious (Freud, 1909d/1953). The epistemic movement is soft but has a great reach, because saying that the infantile is the unconscious leaves these two dimensions in equal circumstances. Thus, the unconscious is the psychic life of the first infancy contained in representations, and we know from that life forgotten by the wit, symptom and the dream.

If it is thus, the question we asked a moment ago would make no sense, it would even be needless, because we could say that our research is about the unconscious. However, we are missing one more piece, which reinforces our thesis on the exploration of the infantile in psychoanalysis as something different than the unconscious. For this we will move again toward the dream, but not only the latent material, but wakefulness.

It is clear that what is repressed by excellence is the infantile incestuous sexuality, and that what is disfigured in the dream are these experiences. Now, this material of wakefulness – before this Freud tells us that it is the repressed infantile – is not only expressed, but it does not have the same texture than the daytime remnants that can also be unconscious. Both, despite being in the dream, don't have the same origin. It is worth mentioning here that the temporarily latent in the dream is pre-conscious, it is closer to consciousness and it can become conscious, the same as the daytime remnants that also meddle in the production of the dream. It is a strange mixture of the repressed infantile past and the current events – wakefulness remnants – with which once again it is proved that the time of the unconscious has nothing to do with the past-present-future categories.

On the unconscious and the infantile

Another difficulty we face lies in the word itself that names this strange memory populated by forgotten memories, that is, the unconscious (*Unbewusste*), because it is used in the descriptive sense, as if it was a system, an agency; and as the unconscious from the dynamic point of view. This last definition had to be introduced as a consequence of the dynamics of repression, for this, it is said that *the repressed is unconscious*, whereas not all that is unconscious is repressed.

There is something in the unconscious that looks to make way toward consciousness while repression, at the same time, is always hunting its off-spring. This repressed material is not only the past, but also the current experiences, the perceptions during wakefulness, for which the unconscious and the repressed infantile are not entirely coincidental. There are other elements that operate in the manifestations of the unconscious and the unconscious itself. It is worth pointing out here that the unconscious does not come in the categories of a classification, because there are no opposites in it, time is not chronological. What lies there according to Freud, are representation-things of the world. In this sense, it is another logic of functioning that is not subjected to consciousness.

Lacan (1987) adds to this that we must locate the unconscious in the dimension of a synchrony. The synchrony shows us, at the same time, the structure in which the extension matters little and the relations-functions give consistency to the elements that contain it, an aspect that is totally related to Freud. Let us see what Freud writes in *The Interpretation of Dreams*: "Strictly speaking, there is no need to assume an actual *spatial* arrangement of the psychic system. It will be enough for our purpose if a definite sequence is established, so that in certain psychic events the system will be traversed by the excitation in a definite *temporal* order" (Freud, 1900a/1953, p. 530).

Both the word *temporal* and the word *spatial* are used in a different meaning than linear space and time. Obligatorily the unconscious cannot be thought as a black box. Regarding this, Lacan would say in 1964, that there is no reason to locate the unconscious as the place for the divinities of the night, there is no reason to think that the unconscious is in a hidden place to which we can access through interpretation to show it to the analysand.

For something to go into memory it must be erased from perception, this is how Freud puts it in his "Letter 52". Then, and taking the example of the presence of the maternal Other, for there to be a representation, the mother must disappear from the child's perception, otherwise there will be of *need* for the representation to be inscribed.

These traces of perception (*Wahrnehmungszeichen*), says Freud in *The Interpretation of Dreams*, must be constituted by simultaneity. Lacan called this synchronic. It is in the diachrony of language, in the signifying succession where the period or the comma stop the eternal reasoning, where a synchronic moment (*après coup*) is produced. From this cut we can read a meaning.

Let us clarify this with the clinic. In the case of the *fort-da*, the child let the wooden reel go and then got it back. That moment was not distressing. Being thus, where could we locate anxiety if it does not come about with the absence of the mother? The anxiety could surface when the mother does not leave and she is always looking after the baby. With a mother like this, there is no need for a signifier that is inscribed in her absence.

Conceiving the world this way has a fracturing effect primarily, because it makes the constancy principle and the pleasure principle fail. Freud mentions that endogenous stimuli, those which he will later call drives, are charges that come from inside the body to later be discharged. This discharge – as we know – is never total. Freud lays out the problems of the drive as that which inhabits the border between the somatic and the psychic. The only thing that appears of the drive are its representatives. The impossibility of the drive's discharge makes the world a place contrary to the pleasure principle.

So, the drive appears as an effect of the signifier. However, the *infans* ("that who does not speak"), due to the tension accumulated, only manages to make an internal modification, for example, a scream or crying, that work as a means of discharge. The functional insufficiency of the body at the beginning of life makes the discharge impossible by there not being another present. The traumatic effects of reality on an apparatus, whose end is to sufficiently discharge tensions, mainly imply two aspects: on one side, the state of discharge of all tension, which would be an equivalent to psychic death; and on the other side, the state of absolute tension.

However, using the energetic metaphor to apprehend the effects of the outer world and those of the drive at the same time has the meaning of overcoming the opposition of the psychic and the external world. Indeed, there is no separation of two heterogeneous fields, but a work of the psychic apparatus and of what reality specifies. We now see the object as a product of the reality principle, the external world as a possibility of the specific act. This means that there is an Other that answers to this child's scream. From that reality principle there is a substitution of the satisfaction movement, because it needs an object that is external to the subject. This principle does not contradict the pleasure principle, but reassures it.

A homeostasis is of the order of the impossible, therefore, the psychic reality appears as the field of the representations born of impossibility, of the psychic fact as a fact of dissatisfaction, of something that is always missing.

Even the pleasure principle, supported by the reality principle, ensures its survival somehow before the attack of both the endogenous and exogenous stimuli. This only happens with the help of someone who is external to it, which most of the times is the mother, as a function. And even the mother must keep a certain distance from the child, because she must leave as well, she must be absent to be named.

The infantile: sexuality and repression

> A *man's maturity* consists in *having found again*
> *the seriousness* one had as a child.
>
> Friedrich Nietzsche, *Beyond Good and Evil*

Does sexuality in a human being have a traumatic face? We can say it does. Sexuality goes through the subject violently and by forcing itself through the subject humanizes him or her. It is important to emphasize that in Freud, it is talked about trauma and not traumatism. We can also accept a distinction as a consequence, because traumatism applies to the external fact that hits the subject (physically), and trauma applies more specifically to the psychic domain (Kaufmann, 2001).

The event of infantile sexuality can exclude, for its own nature, the possibility of a "proper abreaction". Besides, the conditions in which the subject is found influence the moment of the event and also the psychic conflict that prevents the subject to integrate the experience. In Freud, the common factor has an economical nature, the inability of the psychic apparatus to eliminate excitements being the consequence of trauma, according to the constancy principle. As he mentions in Lecture XVIII:

> [. . .] the expression "traumatic" has no other than an economic meaning, and the disturbance permanently attacks the management of available energy. The traumatic experience is one which, in a very short space of time, is able to increase the strength of a given stimulus so enormously that its assimilation, or rather its elaboration, can no longer be effected by normal means.
>
> (Freud, 1916–1917b/1993, p. 252)

In this same lecture, Freud argues that in the analysis of the patient "we may see, by the use of analysis, that in his disease-symptoms and their results he has gone back again into a definite period of his past" (Freud, 1916–1917b/1993), p. 251). Likewise, he mentions in *Studies on Hysteria*: "hysterics suffer mainly from reminiscences" (Freud and Breuer, 1895d/1953, p. 33). He continues in this same way in Lecture XVIII: "[. . .] patients give us the impression of being *fixated* upon some very definite part of their past; they are unable to free themselves therefrom, and have therefore come to be completely estranged both from the present and the future" (Freud, 1916–1917b/1993, pp. 252–253).

Indeed, it is necessary to link the traumatic with sexuality in all its fields with the implications of psychoanalytical treatment, in which Freud insisted from the start by separating sex and sexuality, the same way in which the latter was installed in the subject violently (traumatic).

Before his 1905 text, *Three Essays on the Theory of Sexuality*, Freud had placed human sexuality under a magnifying glass, as well as the short distance that exists between those who were considered normal and those called neurotics, saying: " [. . .] psycho-analysis has demonstrated that there is no fundamental difference, but only one of degree, between the mental life of normal people, of neurotics and of psychotics. A normal person has to pass through the same repressions and has to struggle with the same substitutive structures" (Freud, 1913m/1953, p. 214).

The quote above hits the human being's narcissism, as it was told before, because Freud would enunciate what, according to him, would be the three affronts of humanity. In the first one, earth stopped being the center of the universe. In the second one, man descended from the monkey, not a deity, while in the third, the rational and autonomous me is not the author of itself, but another, indeed, a story which is mostly *unknown to it*.

Contrary to what could be thought at first, Freud did not locate the unconscious as the new center, but it was a *de-centering* from all attempts to locate a concept as a pivot. *In the center there is nothing*. The lack in the Freudian system is put into operation, because without it Freud's entire proposal is not held. The lack of the object mobilizes the elements of said structure.

This inaugurated a new way to read a discourse instituted to be read between lines, a place which the subject sneaks into. The subject is nominated, it is represented, but it is never said what it is. In this sense, we are before a proposal in which the small things (the things left aside since always) reclaim their importance. Forgotten memories, dreams, symptoms, slips, announced the news to the civilized human, announcement in which the subject is unknown or denies the otherness that is updated in the manifestations of the Freudian unconscious.

The framework of the Freudian unconscious is not another element of an epistemology in which the subject (cognoscente) is faced with an object (apprehensible) by the operational definitions of a certain theoretical frame. The Freudian unconscious questions the so-called prehistory of the human (Freud, 1905d/1953, p. 157), it gives way to interrogate it through interpretation (*Deutung*), to cause an effect of meaning. What prevents finding the "total" meaning is directly related to the repressed. And we ask, what is the repressed by excellence? Infantile sexuality.

The infantile is then the anchoring point in this chapter, which cannot be thought without its link to sexuality, or the repression of it. For this, we will directly reference the text quoted earlier, *Three Essays on the Theory of Sexuality*, which can be considered as a nodal point (quilting point) in the Freudian explanation related to praxis and the implication of a sexuality that is not reduced to sexual activity. In this sense, Freud says:

> People have gone so far in their search for high-sounding catch words as to talk of the 'pan-sexualism' of psycho-analysis and to raise the senseless charge against it of explaining 'everything' by sex. [. . .] anyone who looks down with contempt upon psycho-analysis from a superior vantage-point

should remember how closely the enlarged sexuality of psycho-analysis coincides with the Eros of the divine Plato.

(Freud, 1905d/1953, p. 121)

This announcement evidences the neglect of sexuality, and even more, the neglect of a forgotten infantile sexuality. It seems like both in the individual history, as well as in human history, it is not casual to pass by infantile sexuality. Forgetting in certain strata of life produced at that time what Freud called "the psychoneurotics" (Freud, 1905d/1953, p. 159). There was a similitude in the sexuality of this kind of people with that of infants, amnesia being an essential element (in 1905) which gave sexuality the infantile nature.

The example by excellence of psychoneurotics was the figure of the hysteric. She was tormented by the memories that were somehow forgotten which, all the same, organized her existence from another place that wasn't consciousness. The canvas where her lost memories were expressed was her body, but not with a biological character (organs), but a body taken by the word.

Freud listened to the bodies. He did not look at them with the tools of scientific knowledge. Moving away from the medical discourse and established knowledge, he taught us that we do not know anything about the patient and that our knowledge has little or nothing to do with what happens to him or her. *The patient knows more than he or she says.*

Let us contextualize a bit more. This bond of the infantile – in the sense of "the forgotten" – with the hysteric figure goes back to the conversations with Fliess. The issue is addressed in "Letter 84", in which Freud says that what is *experienced sexually* is related to those called psychoneurotics once they become adults and when repression has done its job. Regarding clinical praxis from that period, the objective of the analytical cure was to eliminate the memory lapses. The idea was that the analyst conducted the treatment to reach the forgotten memories and, through the abreaction of excitation, achieve the cathartic effect that would result in the recovery of the memory that the symptom held.

The hypothesis was simple in appearance, they just had to provoke the then "ill patient" to remember aspects of his or her history and start weaving them until he or she reaches the moment in which the traumatic experience happened. Once the person, with the help of the analyst, manages to remember what was apparently forgotten, the symptom would disappear and the cure came as a consequence. Freud puts it this way: "Our therapy works by transforming what is unconscious into what is conscious, and it works only in so far as it is in a position to effect that transformation" (Freud, 1916–1917b/1993, p. 256).

The forgotten infantile was recovered under a sort of regression at the moment in which what has not been processed was left without a non-threatening representation to the ego. What is prevalent in Freudian theory about the dimension of the infantile related to forgetfulness is a (chronological) linear time to which it is possible to return in order to fill the voids of memory. With it, we would aim to a restoration of the memory by erasing amnesia. Contrary to what was pointed out at the beginning of the chapter, we think it is important to highlight these discontinuities in Freudian theory, because it is there where our analysis takes off.

By introducing dimension to the Oedipal conflict and the link with the castration complex, the infantile gets an added value away from a stage or place through which the subject moves and goes on in his or her "development". It is thus that another way to discuss the logical temporal weaving.

Let us see how Freud insists on the organic determination:

> One gets an impression from civilized children that the construction of these dams is a product of education, and no doubt education has much to do with it. But in reality this development is organically determined and fixed by heredity, and it can occasionally occur without any help at all from education.
>
> (Freud, 1905d/1953, p. 161)

It will be interesting to start discovering how far psychoanalysis is from a biological teleology – the dimension of the infantile through which we must go until we reach a moment of fullness (or completeness) in adulthood. This conception would imply, given time, to fill what was lacking in the beginning.

However, we must still explore other ways to be able to approach the infantile regarding other concepts of the Freudian theory. In this sense, we will give a turn of the screw to what was mentioned as "infantile amnesia" in previous lines.

In the same way that Freud picked up infantile amnesia to link it with hysteria, it is necessary to link it with repression, since the infantile is somehow delimited: "[. . .] through the ascertainment that repression has not been constituted completely, yet" (Lévy, 2008, p. 20).

With this approach to the dimension of the infantile, there is still a certain aroma of evolution. If amnesia keeps an intimate relationship with repression, we cannot problematize the infantile related to repression without bearing the symptom in mind. Repression is a clue that Freud leaves us to continue the train of thought in reference to the infantile, not as a phase that we must go through to reach the next level, but as part of the psychic structure.

According to Le Guen (1993), the concept of repression (*Verdrängung*) is shown in several moments in Freud's works. Until before 1895, this concept was linked to a "will to forget", which indicates a motivation to forget the unconscious from 1895 to 1910. Repression appears knotted to the Oedipus complex, the latter being a main axis, because infantile sexuality culminates in its burial, at least in boys, because for the girl the road is another.[2]

But from 1911 to 1919, Freud takes a step forward by writing about the primordial and secondary repression. In 1920, repression goes on to be part of a defense, as a consequence of the discovery of the death drive, without losing its position as a governing axis in psychoanalytical praxis. This explanation does not imply that the concept of repression is described in the same way in Freudian texts; however, this makes its perspective easier. For the moment, we will follow up on the Freud from 1911 to 1919, which allows us to take up on the Oedipal related to the infantile.

Repression is introduced by Freud in 1915 as an intermediate "moment" between the escape from the displeasing stimulus and the adverse or unfavorable judgment (Freud, 1915d/1953). He suggests that before an external stimulus, what follows is escape; however, before an internal and constant stimulus, the impossibility to flee from the ego is decreased. Before the drive motion, another resource is to make a judgment by dismissal. Between these two options is repression as a third, discovered by psychoanalysis. Now, the question would be: what is being repressed??

To approach this question, it is important to first locate the problem. Repression is present before a constant internal stimulus, that is, the drive (*Trieb*). The problem is that according to the results of the research, Freud knew that every satisfaction of the drive is a pleasant one. However, what demands a work of repression is the unpleasant.

The drive motion demands its satisfaction, but in some cases, this satisfaction would cause more displeasure than the pleasure sought. The drive's demand must be set apart from consciousness, which does not imply that it will stop working in the unconscious. This even turns out to be favorable, because from the unconscious it can still work in silence, without being interrupted. To do this job, Freud proposes two moments. The first one is the primordial repression, which consists in denying access to consciousness to the psychic representing agency of the drive; the second, repression properly said. This has the function to hunt down the offspring that through associative links come into contact with the primordially repressed. The primordially repressed "core" also exercises a force of attraction on the offspring (Freud, 1915d/1953).

What has been exposed acquires consistency related to the symptom and repression, since: "Neurotic symptoms also have to have filled this condition (detachment), because they are the offspring of the repressed, which, by means of these formations (symptoms), has ended up overcoming the denied access to consciousness" (Freud, 1915d/1953, p. 145).

In short, repression operates by moving away from consciousness all that appears as displeasing. However, the displeasing, which can be a representation (*Vorstellung*), has another aspect, that of being a representative (*räpresentieren*) of a drive. Freud calls it "amount of affection" (Freud, 1915d/1953, p. 147). This way, we have two dimensions at stake. The drive finds in the amount of affection the representing psychic agency. An example of this transmutation is anxiety.

In this sense, we can understand repression as that which separates the amount of affection (displeasing) of the representation. The amount of affection is knotted to another less threatening representation for the ego. This explains clinically why some experiences, dreams and images can be for certain patients so anguishing, regardless of their harmless nature.

This allows us to take up what we have said about the relationship of infantile and hysterical amnesia. The clearest example of the function of repression is the symptom of conversion, because it definitely pushes away the displeasing representation from consciousness and settles the amount of affection, closing the symptom. This way, the symptom comes to occupy the place of reminiscence, as if the symptomatic formation was the trace in that remembrance, with which the objective is not to force the subject to remember. The memory is present, we just have to know how to read it, listen to it. Resistance is not the enemy to conquer through elucidating interpretations anymore. Resistance to memory has its own meaning (Le Guen, 1993). It is not a stage in the treatment that has to be picked up, because it is present at all times.

In the same way, repression is not in the field of the contingent or temporality; it is there because it is a part of the structure. More than talking about a partial repression in infancy (which would imply partial objects and drives), we would have to talk about adult life, where a sort of total repression with total objects takes place (Lévy, 2008).

It seems that starting with Freud the road to follow is the relationship between the object-choice and the identification. This subjective operation indicates a new form of link with the other, which is going from the object-choice in a first moment, to managing an identification taking from the object a characteristic with which the ego is constituted.

Before focusing on identification, let us look back to what we have exposed so far (sexuality, repression and the infantile). At first there was a coincidence: most of Freud's patients assured that they had suffered a seduction in their infancy from an adult. This adult was regularly close to the family (adult sexuality). In some occasions, it was the child's own parents. Even in the case in which the seducer was another child, the latter would have also been seduced by an adult at first, introducing that child into sexuality before time. As Freud moves forward with his conceptualizations, he proves the sexual origins of neurosis. In every case, disorders of the subject's sexual life (repressed) appear as causes.

This theory of seduction does not constitute a new conceptualization related to the theory of the trauma but its specificity. It is no longer any trauma that causes the amount of quantitative station that psychism cannot elaborate, but specifically the infantile sexual trauma.

In the theory of seduction, Freud will find himself looking for the chronology of seduction, which, according to the moment in which it was experienced, could determine the election of the neurosis. However, it is from "Letter 57" to Fliess that he starts doubting that chronology. And in later works, he reveals his growing findings about the action of fantasy in psychic life. This would lead him to write "Letter 69" in which he "knocks down" the theory of seduction. In it, he confides the following to Fliess: "And now I want to confide in you immediately the great secret that has been slowly dawning on me in the last few months. I no longer believe in my *neurotica*".

We have put quotation marks on "knocks down" because what at first might have been a failure was nothing more than the discovery of the psychic reality, which years later Lacan would locate as a fourth knot in the Borromean chain. Before approaching said proposal, we consider it is necessary to bring up the problem of identification and the signifier, issues that will be worked on next.

Identification and the infantile

"Identification has appeared instead of object-choice" (Freud, 1921c/1953, p. 100). In this same tone, such replacement has little to do with a sequence of phases or stages. The infantile object-choice has a strong link with the object of the adult life. According to Freud, the difference between the infantile sexual life and the adult sexual life is little. The difference lies in the type of relationship with the object of love and the direction of the drives. What calls the attention, according to the identification that replaces the object-choice, is the reference to a subjective movement.

To move on with our objective (the infantile), it is necessary to extend a bond more toward identification. The way in which identification comes in infancy is essential, because it is a part at the same time of both the infant's psychic functioning and structure.

Identifying, in psychoanalysis, is far from *wanting* to be like someone or something in particular. It is not about achieving identity through appearance. It is more in the order of psychology. To talk about identification – in psychoanalysis – it is necessary to abandon the three-dimensional space and situate ourselves somewhere else. Freud created an apparatus of fiction that he called the psychic apparatus. From this atopic invention, identification differs in trying to be seen in phenomena of similitude.

The problem Freud faced was situated – as Nasio mentioned – in locating the subjective operation (unconscious) made by the ego when this was still not established in the child. This identification was frequently seen in praxis when the patient identified with a trait of the lost object. In this Freudian approach, the ego and the object are already constituted.

A five-year-old boy draws his deceased brother who died years earlier. The curious thing is that he draws him wearing his father's shoes (a pair of purple boots) and curly hair on his head. As far as the father goes, he left home. It is evident that the child expresses the traits of both lost objects in the drawing in just one figure. The boy, while playing, says: "my brother watches over me from Heaven, [. . .] I miss him, I used to have curly hair, but I cut it".

As we know, the subversive force of psychoanalysis is precisely to locate in the scene the object forgotten and hidden by scientific discourse. It invites us to not think of identification just from the empiric order. Now, we have to go through the littoral of the word to find what is at stake regarding the subject.

Even from his earliest works, Freud glimpsed that identification appeared in some of his hysteric patients. He initially used the term "identification" in his letters to Wilhelm Fliess, specifically the one from December 17, 1896. A year earlier, the mechanism of identification was described in the case of Elisabeth von R., in *Studies on Hysteria*. Let us remember that Elisabeth von R. took the place (*ersetzen*) of a son and a male friend at the side of her sick father, because he was never able to conceive a boy. This way, Freud aimed to a kind of identification as the "ability" to occupy different psychic positions, that is, like the father so desired, or better put, as her father would have desired to have a son by his side.

By taking the place of an Other, that is, the substitution (*ersatz*) of someone else out of obedience to the father, who assigned that psychic position (*einstellung*) charged with impossibility, Elisabeth von R. is located in a crossroads. She cannot come out of it, "*sie Komme nicht von der stelle*", which could be read as a certain impossibility of her own identity (identification) before her father's desire.

Up to that moment in Freudian theory, identification is understood as the repressed desire to "do as" or "be like", and this is exemplified with the letter to Fliess mentioned earlier. Another place in which Freud worked identification is *The Interpretation of Dreams*, especially with the example of "The Witty Butcher's Wife", which deals with a case of hysterical identification where desire appears as not being satisfied. As it can be seen, when talking about identification and its different modalities, there is another distinction (tacitly implied in elucidations) that seems pertinent to make. We could think of a dimension of identification regarding the subject's constitution and another modality, as presented in clinical praxis.

Freud talks about identification in the process of the subject's constitution more clearly in chapter VII of his *Group Psychology and the Analysis of the Ego*.

He says in the first pages in that part: "Identification is known to psycho-analysis as the earliest expression of an emotional tie with another person" (Freud, 1921c/1953, p. 99).

The function of identification is established in infancy, being at the same time an important trait of the infantile. But in what sense? In the sense that the mother as the thing (*das Ding*), as the first object that the child is a part of, will also be who has the function to be the object that satisfies the infant. Beyond the food she provides, the first representations are also imprinted, such as smells, voices, screams, looks, caresses and, of course, desires.

Now then, what we call the subjective operation of replacement of the object-choice by identification allows us to retake the proposal of the constitution of the infantile not only as a stage. The example that will enable us to go on in this channel is the case of Ida Bauer. Freud analyzes her in the Dora (Ida Bauer) case. In it, he maintains that the object-choice can be transformed by regression in identification. Dora takes from her father a "unique trait" (*der einzinger Zug*). And through a symptom, the cough that her father suffers, makes the incest interdiction present. It is not until 1924 when Freud makes the distinction between identification and the object introjection for the first time.

When the Oedipus complex ends in the boy, the object investitures (introjection) are abandoned and substituted by the identification of the father as signifier. The outlet of the Oedipal complex is, to say it succinctly, where the introjection-identification (*Introjektion-Identifizierung*) alternation stops. An identifying process becomes present through which the boy dis-invests the parental images to identify with "something" of those figures.

Despite all the work Freud makes around identification, he is not satisfied. However, he would later rescue it having been able to locate the superego instance, which he considered a sort of identification achieved with the parental instance.

In the boy, he proposes the superego instance as the culmination and the dissolution of the Oedipal complex. This is what has given the boy's identification with the punitive and/or forbidding instances, for which he no longer needs someone to tell him that he is wrong, but he will sanction himself.

Other fields linked with said identifications are the ones that work as those that support the ego. The last center that the cosmos had was the ego. Now we know that the ego is not autonomous, it is not origin, there is not even an ego that is born as the organic boy is. The ego is essentially identification.

When Lacan talked about *das Ding* as the trace left by the real mother, he allows the reading that the trait with which the subject identifies is the radical absence of that which the mirror cannot reflect. The real leaves its face (or trace) in memory, which, despite being forgotten, still affects.

The memory constructed with the representations that influence on the ego, which, right until before Freud we considered as the author of itself, dwells in the unconscious. The implication of this modality of thought opens the door to elucidating a work of thought, which adjusts to what for a long time was considered as refuse (the dream, for example). For Freud, the relationship of repression with the unconscious is essential, when he proposes that: "Everything that is repressed is unconscious; but we cannot assert that everything unconscious is repressed" (Freud, 1923b/1953, p. 19). With this, by not being empirically provable, we are left with only some traces that we can follow.

The curious thing is that the infantile, besides being repressed, leaves evidence in the subject of all the history of that psychic reality, which even by being repressed it manages to sort the barrier to be heard (dream, wit, symptom, slip). This way, *not everything that is unconscious is infantile, but everything that is infantile has become unconscious*.

We face an old problem of psychoanalysis: the place. It has become very complex not to think of the unconscious from the obviousness of the in-out couple, reason for which Lacan, in Book 9 of *The Seminar*, opens the spatial complexity problematized from topology. He states: "Because it is a question of topology and not of metrical properties, the question of the greater length of one side with respect to the other has no significance. That it is not this which interests us, because it is the reciprocal function of these circles that it is a matter of utilizing" (Lacan, 1961).

The unconscious must not be sought, it appears. It cannot be announced either, only enunciated. The place of the unconscious lies in the act of talking or forgetting. The structure is lacking since always, on the contrary there would be no structure or its characteristics.

Let us remember that the unconscious is located by Lacan between the registers of the symbolic and the imaginary. On the side of the symbolic, he placed death, and on the side of the imaginary, he placed the body.[3]

Part II

Nachträglich: the a posteriori as instant of signification

> [. . .] there are certain elements which are not intended to be interpreted (or read, as the case may be) but are only designed to serve as 'determinatives' that is to establish the meaning of some other element.
>
> Sigmund Freud, *The Claims of Psychoanalysis to Scientific Interest*
> (Freud, 1913/1993)

In psychoanalysis, we cannot think of a linear time; that was the great Freudian discovery. To understand this proposal, let's look back at what we mentioned about trauma in some paragraphs above: for an experience to be traumatic it is necessary that there is a second moment.

Juan, aged six, was witness to a fight between his parents. The father suffered psychotic episodes in which he assured he was being followed and that his wife cheated on him with other men. One night, during an argument with her, he stabbed her. Her parents arrived at the apartment, which was just above theirs. The man was mad and was shouting that they would kill him. The grandmother ran to the room and saw Juan crying next to the wall while saying: "my dad killed my mom". The boy's father stabbed himself several times. When the ambulance arrived, they could just save the father, the mother had died. The grandfather, who was the one who asked for the interview, told this story.

Juan came into the office and when asked who had brought him there, he answered without doubting: "my mom". When asked for her name, he just answered: "I can't remember".

The scene that this boy witnessed is very hard, but not only because of that is it traumatic. It is necessary to have a S_2, that is, a second moment, to try to make sense of the first one. In this case, the treatment pointed to recovering the methodical traces from that night to elaborate as much as possible on that experience.

What is new and interesting about the Freudian proposal is thinking about time at the side, a linear temporal mark, just as we think it from common sense. With this innovation, the symptoms that seemed to make no sense recover some logic.

In Lectures XVII and XVIII, Freud provides several examples that reveal the importance of deciphering the symptom. For this, it is necessary to underline logical time, in other words, the resignification (*nachträglich*). He also mentions some examples of patients, like the women with a ritual for before they go to bed or senseless habits. Once the first scene is recovered (past) in the present (second scene), the symptom has no more reason to be.

Freudian writing is plagued with comings and goings, which does not necessarily imply setbacks. It is not about going after the development of an idea. Complications happen in a particular way of research where we take a unique clinical case as a referent of a mechanism. This writing takes the description of a clinical case in function of the causal explanation, that is, it does not stay on the level of the description in the sense of phenomenology. In this sense, Álvarez, Esteban and Sauvagnat say:

> [. . .] the importance given to the ways in which the elements that conform the structure relate, before considering that said elements possess an intrinsic value; the transcendence of language and its structuring power of subjectivity, which allows an articulation of the structure in function to the relations and the places (topology).
>
> (Álvarez, Esteban and Sauvagnat, 2004, p. 146)

The importance of language beyond its implication as a means to communicate becomes evident. What Freud inaugurates is language in its right dimension as a constituent of a subject inserted into a historical and social context. This idea goes back to his early work, in which he suggests the possibility of a *linguistic association* that is related to memory. In this case we know that the memory that is listened to is not the memory of historical facts.

The polymorphous perverse in Freud

One of the figures that scandalized the nineteenth and twentieth centuries was the Freudian polymorphous perverse. In this concept, education and good habits are knotted with what psychoanalysis has showed us concerning the existence of the drive in the sexualized subject. Freud considered that the child, compared to the adult, has an undifferentiated sexuality, which moves around a change of goal in the drive and is aimed toward an asexual end. This way, perversion is not a state in which the subject evolves, but it has been an inhibition in the constitution.

Although the child can be called a polymorphous perverse, it is in function of an ideal that functions as a referent, an ideal that has a first and last name, as is the adult.

History has shown that sexual deviations (*pervertere*) result obscene in relation to an ideal of sexual exercise. Freud states that the human being possesses a polymorphous perverse disposition, that is, the human being, despite choosing a sexual object, has a certain disposition to bisexuality (or deliberate sexuality) in which "something" is repressed.

Even though we are used to the word "perversion" having a strong echo due to the hints that everyday language has given it, the Latin etymology of the word points to perversion having to do with "turning around, destroy or transform", whereas polymorphous (from the Greek *poly-* and *morphe*) means "with many forms", therefore, this Freudian term is understood as the multiple forms for turning (or thinking) sexuality.

The polymorphous perverse child's sexuality in Freud makes a reference to the drives that are not in the dominion of sexual activity yet, a state in which the father of psychoanalysis suggested the teleological possibility of a gathering of the drives toward an end. This is a teleological proposal in which reproduction would be the end. However, this point of view can be re-thought and re-assessed.

This new reading about a child's perverse sexuality acquires a greater strength afterwards, for example, in the article "The Infantile Genital Organization", which functions as a complement to *Three Essays on the Theory of Sexuality* from 1905. There he announces that the so-called perversion, which is not related to degeneration, plays a very important role in the child's constitution, because through denial, the boy does not accept that his mother has no penis, therefore, she is not lacking and as a consequence, he is also complete.

The mother plays a fundamental role both for the boy and for the girl, being the first object of love. Likewise, the polymorphous perverse disposition is linked to the encounter of the anatomical difference of the sexes and its consequences in each one of their structuring.

Thus, Freud rescues perversion from the ranks of psychiatry. It is not treated as an illness anymore, but as the position that the child occupies before what should be. Likewise, the child's polymorphous perversion is now the stage in which drives look to be satisfied separately. The law and the limits it implies still come from the outside.

By not being an abnormality anymore, but part of the child's constitution, the polymorphous perverse sexuality does nothing more than accent the drive and its movement in a horseshoe shape, as Lacan proposes in Book XI of *The Seminar*. And the mother – as the Other – by being the one who gives the signifier mediates this movement. Perverse is not degenerate, but another way to be positioned before the Other's demand.

The reading of the mother-son relationship and the child = phallus equation

What we exposed earlier allows us to accent the idea that in Freud the mother's function is central inasmuch as it is her who libidinizes the infant.

In a start, Freud formulated that it was adults who eroticized children, as if the infant was a passive being and allowed to be invested by the adult. From this theory, he expresses a first attempt to explain neuroses: it is not something factual, but what he called fantasy, of which the adult, as the incarnation of the Other in the story, does nothing but mediate desire.

According to Rodulfo (2006), it is possible to think of the infant not only from the position as desired or undesired, but under the coordinates: desired for what or by whom? Or, undesired for what or by whom? Questions that broaden the panorama and make the mother-son relationship complex.

In Freud, the place of the child functions as one of the outlets or solutions to the Oedipus in the woman. This symbolic equivalence has in itself all of the properties that Lacan located in the signifier. Beyond thinking it as a simple change, Freud gives us the opportunity to find the metaphor in this symbolic child = phallus movement. How is this?

For the mother, a way to come out of the Oedipus is by making the child = phallus equivalence. The phallus symbolically represents the lack in the Other, that is, the phallus is a signifier (void of meaning) that represents the lack. From this perspective it is evident that the mother, who somehow phallicizes the infant, invests him or her with the ideal of the ego, libidinizes him or her via the Other, that is, invests him or her with the history of which she is the spokesperson.

Now well, the boy is wanted to be the bearer of the symptom in the family. He will be located in that position before the Other, the mother and the father, the grandparents, and so forth. So, the positions that Rodulfo proposes and that we pick up to take a step forward are the child in the position of the phallus (imaginary and symbolic), of the symptom and specter.[4]

It is precise to clarify that the dimension of the *specter* can be also thought as an equation. Contrary to the child = phallus equation, the child positioned as he who comes to occupy the place of a dead sibling, uncle or aunt, or relative, implies the denial of the event (a sort of melancholy), which means arriving into a family and occupy a different place in the signifying chain of the family history, making the equivalence where the dead is linked to the living. Idea that we will work further on:

> In an identical denial of the child as an event, the core structuralist postures incur, involuntarily, in which the being that is born is reduced to unleash the pre-existing and occupy a locker in the family myth without altering it, through what Derrida calls "the ongoing work of difference".
>
> (Rodulfo, 2006, p. 239)

This is an example of an equivalence to precisely look after the presence of death at the expense of someone's existence, or it could be said, doing whatever is necessary for the structure, the family history, stays unmodified. This is a way for the dead person to stay and the living person to occupy his or her place, with the guilt (or not) that this may imply.[5]

It is here where what was developed in the chapter acquires consistency, to be weaved at the time of the writing. The position of the child as the phallus has a strong presence in the work of Freud, because, as we said earlier, it was one of the possible solutions to the Oedipus in the woman. Phallicizing the child allows making him or her a metaphor, include a new signification. The arrival of a new infant to the family somehow implies resignifying the stories weaved around him or her canceling the linear temporality at the same time that the logical or retroactive time (*nachträglich*) becomes present, which introduces due to its delayed effect, an out of time in the diachrony, that is, synchrony, inaugurating a different movement.

So, that couple, regardless of their sex, must occupy the place of the father and mother, but not of their own parents, but a different one that gives meaning to the new member. This way, the symbolic equivalence of the phallicized child does not come to occupy the place of the phallus as a hinge between the sexes, but as an articulator of both *partenaires* before the function of the self, which – as we know – is to function as a bond between the nonexistent relationship (proportion) between the sexes. At the same time that this discontinuity is pointed out, it is more evident that the child only comes to occupy a place in desire, in the parents' lack. This "privileged" place must be abandoned to try having that which is valuable to the parents' eyes, the phallic (*fallus*, insignia), with nothing more to do but stop being it. *Stop being the phallus to seek having it.*

Later we will talk about the difference between the position that the child takes and the phallus (whether imaginary or symbolic). For now, it is convenient to add that for a father or mother to take the child as a phallus (symbolic, in this case), as that which will continue what they did not do, his castration is also necessary. Why? Because thinking of the child as their own continuation implies assuming that they are mortal, accepting their own death and, therefore, taking a position: castration. Only by implicitly accepting death itself, a mother or father can have a phallicized child and not as an object of enjoyment.

In the cases of the child as a phallus (imaginary or symbolic), as well as in the cases in which he or she is a symptom or specter, it is possible to say that the child is not an individual or a mind, but a place within the structure.

To conclude, we can mention a scene from the film *Abel*. In it, we see how a child committed to a psychiatric hospital and who never speaks acquires a position when he gets home, where his siblings live too, and his mother asks him to go with her to a parents meeting at school. It is this way that Abel takes the place of the husband for the mother and father for his siblings. Abel is finally eloquent and acts normally when he takes a position in the family and the others assign that place. What opens these possibilities in this boy are not the drugs or therapies, but a position in the family.

When a child comes to consultation we can say that he or she is "ill" as an effect of holding the family just like it is, that is, to keep it unharmed. The child is the scapegoat of family tension. We will then see that in a delirium, a phobia or an obsessive behavior, there will be an unsatisfied couple, a cursed inheritance from the grandfather or a maddening father.

In the case of the child as a symptom, the analyst will have to bear in mind that his or her intervention will modify the coordinates of this family, as a result of this intervention, the balance will change, re-distributing the tension of dissatisfaction in the other members. These members will be able, at the same time, to assume their quota of tension or go to an expert, because "the psychoanalyst is not doing things right".

Notes

1 To make a first note, we will follow Esteban Levin (2006) on the difference he proposes between the terms "infancy" and "infantile" in his book *¿Hacia una infancia virtual? La imagen corporal sin cuerpo*. He says: "Infancy ends, finishes with no return, but the infantile that is instituted there remains in time" (p. 12). This clarification answers to the reader not having to be surprised of not finding the term "infancy" in this chapter. In

chapter 4 we will take up this quote to specify said difference in relation to language and the word according to Jean-François Lyotard and Giorgio Agamben, so as to begin the tour of what we consider as structuring in the subject, at the moment in which it bespeaks language and, at the same time, surfaces in the interdictum.

2 It is Lacan who, in order to come out of the apparent crossroads, will put the castration complex as the true agent of the subject's constitution, leaving the Oedipus complex as fantasy.

3 The knot missing in the "Joyce case" lies in a knotting between these two resisters, where the ego has the function of knotting the structure. The ego is assimilated by Lacan as the Freudian *Lust-Ich*, in which he underlines that this "me-pleasure" is not related between an inside and an outside. The infant does not have a distinction between what belongs to it and what does not. Let us remember that this "me-pleasure" is linked to the mother figure and, therefore, to *das Ding*.

4 The term "specter" is mine. It is also necessary to reiterate the clarification that it is not the "phantom" that Lacan proposes.

5 The most famous case of this position is Eugenio Salvador Felipe Jacinto Dalí, better known as Salvador Dalí. Dalí's brother, who was also named Salvador Dalí, died when he was seven due to an attack of meningitis. Another two famous cases of having the same name as a dead sibling are Argentinian writer Ernesto Sábato and painter Vincent van Gogh.

Bibliography

Álvarez, J. M., Esteban, R. and Sauvagnat, F. (2004). *Fundamentos de psicopatología psicoanalítica*. Madrid: Síntesis.

Borges, J. L. (1980). Nueva refutación del tiempo. *Prosa Completa 2*. Barcelona: Bruguera.

Dolto, F. (1977). *Lettre de l'ecole freudienne de Paris*. Paris: Gallimard.

Dolto, F. (1984). *La Imagen Inconsciente del Cuerpo*. Buenos Aires: Paidós.

Freud, S. (1895d/1953). *Studies on Hysteria. S. E.*, *2*. London: Hogarth.

Freud, S. (1905c/1953). *Jokes and Their Relation to the Unconscious. S. E.*, *8*. London: Hogarth.

Freud, S. (1905d/1953). *Three Essays on the Theory of Sexuality. S. E.*, *7*. London: Hogarth.

Freud, S. (1905e/1953). *Fragment of an Analysis of a Case of Hysteria. S. E.*, *7*. London: Hogarth.

Freud, S. (1909d/1953). *Notes Upon a Case of Obsessional Neurosis. S. E.*, *10*. London: Hogarth.

Freud, S. (1913/1993). El interés por el psicoanálisis. *Obras Completas Tomo XIII*. Amorrortu editores: Buenos Aires.

Freud, S. (1913m/1953). *On Psychoanalysis. S. E.*, *12*. London: Hogarth.

Freud, S. (1915d/1953). *Repression. S. E.*, *14*. London: Hogarth.

Freud, S. (1916–1917/1953a). *A General Introduction to Psychoanalysis*. Conference XIII: Archaic Remnants and Infantilism in the Dream. *S. E.*, *15*. London: Hogarth.

Freud, S. (1916–1917/1953b). *A General Introduction to Psychoanalysis*. Conference XVIII. Traumatic Fixation – The Unconscious. *S. E.*, *15*. London: Hogarth.

Freud, S. (1921c/1953). *Group Psychology and the Analysis of the Ego. S. E.*, *18*. London: Hogarth.

Freud, S. (1923b/1953). *The Ego and the Id. S. E.*, *19*. London: Hogarth.

Freud, S. (1950a/1953). *Project for a Scientific Psychology. S. E.*, *1*. London: Hogarth.

Freud, A. (1989). *Normality and Pathology in Childhood: Assessments of Development*. London: Karnac Books.

Harari, R. (1990). *Fantasma: Fin de Análisis?* Buenos Aires: Nueva Visión.

Joyce, J. (2006). *Retrato del artista adolescente*. México: Ediciones Coyoacán.

Kaufmann, P. (2001). *Elementos para una enciclopedia del psicoanálisis*. Buenos Aires: Paidós.

Klein, M. (1990). El desarrollo de un niño. *Obras Completas. Amor, Culpa y Reparación, 1*. Buenos Aires: Paidós.

Lacan, J. (1961). *El Seminario. Libro 9. La identificación*. Buenos Aires: GAMA Producción Gráficas SRL.

Lacan, J. (1965). *El Seminario. Libro 14. La Lógica del Fantasma*. Buenos Aires: GAMA Producción Gráficas SRL.

Lacan, J. (1982). *El Seminario. Libro 1. Los escritos técnicos de Freud*. Buenos Aires: Paidós.

Lacan, J. (1984). L´Étourdit. *Ecansión 1*. Buenos Aires: Paidós.

Lacan J. (1987). *El Seminario. Libro 11. Los Cuatro Conceptos Fundamentales del Psicoanálisis*. Buenos Aires: Paidós.

Lacan, J. (1999). *El Seminario. Libro 5. Las formaciones del inconsciente*. Buenos Aires: Paidós.

Lacan, J. (2005). Dos Notas Sobre el Niño. *Intervenciones y Textos 2*. Buenos Aires: Manantial.

Lacan, J. (2009a). Función y Campo de la palabra y el lenguaje en psicoanálisis. *Escritos 1*. México: Siglo XXI.

Lacan, J. (2009b). *El Mito Individual del Neurótico*. Buenos Aires: Paidós.

Le Guen, C. (1993). *La represión*. Buenos Aires: Amorrortu.

Levin, E. (2006). *Hacia una infancia virtual? La imagen corporal sin cuerpo*. Buenos Aires: Nueva Visión.

Lévy, R. (2008). *Lo infantil en psicoanálisis*. Buenos Aires: Letra Viva.

Lunger, V. (2005). El Discurso y *Die Verneinung*. In: Benjamín Domb, Norberto Ferreyra, Roberto Harari, Víctor Lunger, Hugo Levin and Isidoro Vegh. *Seminario de lectura de Los Escritos Técnicos de Freud de Jacques Lacan*. Buenos Aires: Letra Viva.

Miller, J.-A. (1987). *Escisión, Excomunión, Disolución. Tres momentos en la visa de Jacques Lacan*. Buenos Aires: Manantial.

Peusner, P. (2006). *Fundamentos de la Clínica Lacaniana con Niños*. Buenos Aires: Letra Viva.

Rodulfo, R. (2006). *El niño y el significante*. Buenos Aires: Paidós.

Roudinesco, E. and Plon, M. (1998). *Diccionario de Psicoanálisis*. Barcelona: Paidós.

Seattle, H. (2005). *Palabra y Silencio en Psicoanálisis*. México: UAM-Xochimilco.

Segal, H. (2006). *Introducción a la Obra de Melanie Klein*. Barcelona: Paidós.

Winnicott, D. (1971). *Playing and Reality*. London: Tavistock Publications.

Winnicott, D. (2001). *Collected Papers: Through Paediatrics to Psycho-Analysis*. London: Tavistock Publications.

Yannick, F. (1990). *Francoise Dolto: De la Ética a la Práctica del Psicoanalisis en Niños*. Buenos Aires: Nueva Vision.

Chapter 3

The Lacanian subject

Notes for considering the place and function of the child in psychoanalysis

In the image, lack of awareness; in the word, acknowledgement; in silence, the event.

Once we have delimited our posture regarding what we understand as the infantile in psychoanalysis and developed an introduction about the importance of the subject, it is necessary to point out the importance that it has in Lacan, as well as its impact in science, philosophy and psychoanalysis. Lacan has also observed how for some of Freud's contemporaries, and even for some of the post-Freudians (Melanie Klein, Anna Freud, Donald Winnicott), the subject went unnoticed. We know that the problems of the subject do not arise with psychoanalysis; however, there is a subversion with the revolution spearheaded by Freud. It is finally Lacan who aims the problem to where the subject appears and vanishes.

There are many texts that problematize the subject. This is because there is no signifier that says what the subject is; it distinguished itself by its lack in being. The only way to be able to locate it is language, which represents it before another signifier. This trait does not leave the child forgotten, that is to say, the child is also subjected to language.

In the last chapter we said that the child was the effect of a structure. So let us take one step forward and say that the child is an effect of his or her structure. With this advance we intend to locate said structure in a singularity. It is not just about a structure, but a very specific one in which the child is captured by his or her phantom. When saying "his or her structure", we emphasize not the structure of his or her belonging, but that of which he or she is an effect and where his or her singularity dwells in respect to others, even his or her siblings.

The subject (the silence) of the unconscious as an event

Hard sciences have thought the human under the logic of linearity, a cause with an effect without discontinuity. Facing this, what follows is to look for a beginning and, as a consequence, a goal or an end. In this sense, the trend has been to look for answers before formulating questions. The focus has been placed on linear coincidences evoked by biological disciplines, with a tendency to development and evolution. This has had as a consequence the concealing of what is important in psychoanalysis, that is, the subject.

In many of his texts, Freud resorts to development thinking that at some point psychoanalysis can be explained from chemistry and biology, and hoping to find the answer to psychic processes in chemistry. This is an issue that, on the other hand, scientists have been obstinate in deciphering, because today what we are looking for are the cancer and obesity genes, and the brain cells that keep traumatic memories, or for the parts of the brain that intervene in certain specific processes. These attempts seem to be a great progress where past and present come together and a promising future is projected.

However, such escalated debates still have not accounted for the question on hand, i.e., the subversion of the subject. If we could define the subject, there would be no more history. But what do we understand by *subject*? If there was a word in language that said what it *is*, then we would be able to think of a perfect development of such a subject, a circle that closes perfectly on itself and a developmental logic would then be the answer. And like every answer, it would aim to a certainty (albeit an imaginary one?) that will perfectly close the circle, leading to a concordance.

Fortunately, our bet is not found there. We are challenged to play in the knowing that no system is complete. This lack allows and makes it possible for these systems to have mobility. The structuring of the human is then due to the links we create with others. So, the lacks, the failures and the impossibility are what throw us (in psychoanalysis) into building ourselves in our relationships with others. In this way, according to what we have been working so far, the structure itself announces that something is missing. In other words, to think about the structure expecting an answer about what the subject *is* will be misleading, what we propose is to build questions about the subject's position in the unconscious and, in a certain way, in culture through thinking the structure.

The question then, is not: "To be, or not to be, that is the question" but "to be or not, to be that is the question". By moving the comma from the "to be" to the "not", the sentence stops inviting to the suspension in the action and, on the contrary, announces an enigma that incites the subject's movement. Let us stress the second part, which is "to be that is the question". We can think this as the being that is being as it is being told. Curiously enough, the "being" of the subject is not in the signifying chain. That is how the subject makes its appearance in history, in philosophy and psychoanalysis.

The question of the subject goes through all of Lacan's work. Although it does not appear in Freud as clearly as it does in Lacan, it can be read as a concept and it can be seen that its subversion is announced under the logic of the unconscious. We know that the issue of the subject is not a new one. Descartes, Hegel and Freud talked about it at some point; however, it is Lacan who takes the time to clear the bonds between one thought and the other.

Even though Descartes does not use the word *subject*, but *ego* (I), there is an implication of the human being (cogitation), of itself as *res cogitans*. But why bother in using one word and not the other? Because the reach they have must be considered in its just dimension. And which is that dimension? The signifier. If we talk about the individual, we reference the indivisible and if something is indivisible there is no fracture. If we say human being, we include the *being* in the game and as we know, the *being* cannot be defined. Metaphysics is in charge of that study. Psychoanalysis is not metaphysics. If we say person, we reference a mask, since the etymology of person means precisely that.

On the other hand, the word "subject" has many readings. One of them points out that the subject is subjected to language. In psychoanalysis it is not about talking of the "subject" as a synonym of the "guy". We don't give meaning to the phrase "there goes that guy (subject)", but we try to locate it in respect to language and the unconscious. We have a subject of the unconscious that is not a substance. Talking of the subject in psychoanalysis is more related to the *sujet* (in French), which references the topic or ideal of which we talk.

A proposal based on psychoanalysis that does not include the dimension of the Freudian discovery is unsustainable, both the absence of the object as well as the stage in which this is played, that is, the unconscious. Although Freud did not propose the structure as a concept, we can trace the possibilities of thinking it *a posteriori*.

The Freudian unconscious is not a black box; it has a logic and a structure. It is a conscience underneath another one, but a memory of which the subject has no knowledge and that, however, appears affecting the speaker's acting and saying. In Freud, the unconscious has a place (topic) with no bodily location, that is why he invented the concept of psychic apparatus. Lacan, on the other hand, was forced to go to other disciplines such as logic and topology to capture the unconscious beyond the Freudian representational models.

Indeed, the unconscious is not within the inside-outside localization. It functions under the differential operations of the signifier. Here is where the subverted – and why not, subversive – subject appears in psychoanalysis. What is interesting is that the subject is said to "have appeared", always in the past. We never say: "it will appear here or there". In Heideggerian terms, the subject is shown to be *fading*.

To elucidate the panorama, let us consider the subject of science, not the subject of which we talk, but the one we investigate. That one faced with the object in search of a knowledge that coincides with the truth. In epistemology, the subject wants to know the object, and this place of the object can also be occupied by another subject. The problem is that to be able to know the object – whichever it is – it must first be defined by the subject that investigates.

The so-called objectivity is pierced by subjectivity, there is no outlet. This failed relationship evidences that the model of epistemology dreams of a concordance between the subject and the object, terms that will never coincide, since the object is not the Thing (*das Ding*) – nothing can be said of it, it is outside all signifying referent – and the subject is not the I, the place of identifications.

Let go a little further revisiting Descartes's ideas. The subject of the unconscious is not the Cartesian ego, even though there is a link between them. The bond that allows us to think these dimensions will be doubt and certainty (*Gewissheit*). In that gap we will locate the unconscious that lacks to make knowledge something complete and truth something that is impossible to say in whole.

In the second part of the *Discourse on Method*, Descartes proposes to tear from his spirit all those ideas that he has been taught. The complexity of this principle lies in the equivalence that he makes between reason, the spirit, the ego and the soul. The difference lies in being as a consequence of an "I" that doubts while thinking. However, we are not talking here about perfect being, since doubting to know announces a lack. On the other hand, Descartes thinks of the existence of God as someone who knows without doubting, which evidences a perfect being (Descartes, 2008). He says: "I concluded that it couldn't be a perfection in God to be composed of these two natures – the intellectual and the bodily – and consequently that he was not composed of them" (Descartes, 2008, p. 25).

Descartes appeals to God to locate truth in its place. Even reason is not an element that can announce the truth of the human being. Reason itself does not dictate what is true or false, it only accentuates that truth is not on the side of whoever doubts. Certainty, evidently, is doubt itself. In this sense, by being the ego who doubts and by doubting everything transmitted by the senses, Descartes accepts it an otherness. Therefore, he thinks, and thinking is being. The next step is answering the question: "Who am I?" The answer is: "A thing that thinks. What is that? A thing that doubts, understands, affirms, denies, wills, refuses, and that also imagines and senses" (Descartes, 2008, p. 67).

The *res cogitans* is not an object or attribute that can be named or even imagined. The thinking thing does not go through the register of the imaginary to be represented. It can only be grasped through reason. With such an approach, Descartes begins his *Discourse on Method*. He says that "good sense", that is, reason, "is the best-shared thing in the world" (Descartes, 2008, p. 67).

According to these ideas, reason functions as a point of support to knowing. There is no other way, because the senses trick us. In this sense, the Cartesian ego is defined by what is not, since it is not a breeze, wind or other thing. All the elements of the world that we can imagine to name the *res cogitans* can be doubted. The definition does not go to the register of the phenomenological, it only refers to the thinking act itself. The Cartesian human being knows of its cognizance, but does not possess the representation of something that could provide any indication of its *being*.

The subject that Descartes talks about as the ego lacks representation insofar as its being is concerned. Thinking (*cogito*) equally lacks representation and, at the same time, as curious as it seems, it is Archimedes's point to mobilize the rest of the representations.

How is it possible that the *cogito* is excluded from the same act that implies it, it being the center of the universe of the classical period? Without intending to make equivalences between Cartesian ideas and psychoanalysis, we may think that the act that implies doubting announces what we have been working so far, that is, the unconscious. Evidently, Descartes did not contemplate such dimension in his epistemological scheme.

We could try to go further and say that the subject in psychoanalysis is going through doubt, in the same way as the Cartesian ego. This going through is an effect of something that is missing in language to compensate for the gap. The subverted subject is not the one that thinks, but the one that is "thought", or to put it more clearly, the subject is said, it does not say.

Lacan does not go to the subject of science or criticize the *cogito* to disqualify it, but to confirm the Freudian ideas. There is no center of the universe. The *res cogitans* is not the axis under which we can problematize and solve the division between knowing and truth, because the discordant element is the unconscious' certainty.

However, the field opened by Descartes and his idea "I think, therefore I am" announces the rupture of the bond with God and inaugurates man's time. He does not deny God's existence; however, he states that it is not necessary to go to Him, or to something out of the soul (I) to be able to formulate questions.

There is still an element missing to be able to size the Cartesian and Freudian doubt, as well as the impact that they both had in modernity. It is necessary to rescue the subject from epistemology. Before the question: "what can be known?" we had mentioned that the subject has a place, because it is facing the object. It is an active subject that seeks to know. Reading Freud, Lacan, for his part, faces the subject to a remainder of itself. The subject in psychoanalysis does not face the object, because it is lost.

Regarding epistemologies, they all look to answer how to give knowledge to the subject, or as Kant asked: what can be known? Whether through experience or reason. For psychoanalysis, it is not primordial to achieve a knowledge alien to the subject. Whoever goes to analysis will not learn more as if he or she was going to school. The knowledge that is agreed upon in the analytical device is of the unconscious. A teenage analysand says: "I always knew I was adopted, something in me knew. Now that I say it, I have the feeling that I always knew, I don't know why I am surprised . . ."

As mentioned by this analysand, the knowledge of which he talks is not new. The signifiers that guide his life through the staging of the phantom are not external to him, and it is not the analyst either who implants them in order to achieve some subjective movement through suggestion; therefore, the subject subjected to a history (language) does not look to know the truth, unlike the epistemological model that points to the encounter between the divided subject and the lost object.

But the concept of the subject – as we have seen – does not appear in Descartes. So, where does the idea of the subject come from? From Freud, it appears; however, he does not problematize it. It is Lacan who goes to the philosophy of historical materialism to bring a tool into psychoanalysis with which to theoretically grasp – as much as possible – the appearance of the unconscious in the clinical device.

With the problematization of the subject as something that is different from the Freudian ego, the dimension of the symbolic is inaugurated, and with it, the rest of the registers (real and imaginary). In this sense, Lacan goes to Hegel to account for the subject, because he is who introduces negativity more clearly in philosophy. We had seen that something had strained into the Cartesian *cogito*, since that something was nothing that we could represent in us; however, it was Hegel who gave Lacan that tool to introduce the word as founding.

Descartes says: "I am, I exist, but what I am?" And he himself answers: something that thinks (*res cogitans*). Hegel answers: "I am not only a thinking being. I am the bearer of an absolute Knowledge. And this Knowledge is actually, at the moment when I think, incarnated in me. Therefore, I am not only a thinking being; I am also – and above all – Hegel. What then, is this Hegel?" (Kojève, 1990, pp. 173–174).

With this last question he opens the possibility to think the subject from its historical contexts and, therefore, linked to language. Descartes does not use these categories, or he doubts them, because when we think denying everything that the senses might capture, we put aside history and its discontinuities. Let us now see a quote in which Kojève knits thinking and the word, and with this, the subject.

> Before analyzing the "*I think*", before proceeding to the Kantian theory of *knowledge* – i.e., of the relation of the relation between the (conscious) *subject* and the (conceived) object, one must ask what this subject is that

is revealed in and by the *I* of "I think". One must ask when, why and how man is led to say "I . . .".

(Kojève, 1990, p. 176)

Without fear of being wrong, we can assert that the action through which someone is led to say I is directly related to the I (*je*) that Lacan proposes, as an effect of the mirror stage, and to the function of that *shifter* in the articulation of the signifiers. Later on, Kojève says: "For there to be Self-Consciousness, there must – first of all – be Consciousness. In other words, there must be revelation of Being by Speech" (Kojève, 1990, p. 176).

This is the pre-text that Lacan needed to introduce the subject in its dimension of "represented" by the signifier. The event of the modern subject announces the death of God (the Other is lacking), with which there is no center anymore, the universe is not circular. Even Freud does not place the unconscious as a new center.

Hegel thinks of the final synthesis or absolute self-consciousness as a historical point of arrival. For psychoanalysis this is of the order of the impossible, because the subject cannot access absolute consciousness of itself.

This can be thought from another perspective of psychoanalysis where the I is not the subject, and the subject is not the one that is founded on the action where it thinks. Sometimes, when the subject thinks-doubts (*cogito*), it is surprised by saying something that does not go through its will and goes beyond itself. The subject is said.

On the other hand, the I, as a place of synthesis, asks no questions. Freud thought about it as part of a topic, as an effect of the detachment of the id. If this is so, the ego is not the author of itself, it is an effect of something external. Indeed, it is Lacan who locates it in its function of a place of unknowingness. As far as the subject goes, it asks, investigates, it is said by the unconscious, and when the unconscious appears, it leaves the subject in a bad place. The ego as a place of synthesis comes to give a (hesitant) answer to the question: where is the signifier that comes to say what the subject is? The ego answers, but not flawlessly, saying: "I".

The 'I' is not there at the beginning, and this is precisely what the ego ignores. When a boy is asked: how many brothers and sisters do you have? He answers from his place as a subject: I have three. John, Peter and I. This example, besides allowing us to think the function of the signifier, shows that the ego and the subject are exclusive between them. The subject speaks and is outside of language, whereas the ego is an effect of the image and is traceable in the signifying chain, or, in the reflection.

Based on these questions, Lacan problematizes the subject's subversion. In his article "The Subversion of the Subject and the Dialectic of Desire in the Freudian Unconscious", Lacan gives back the subject its status in psychoanalytical epistemology and takes the time necessary to tell us that his subject is not the Cartesian ego, or Hegelian self-consciousness (*Selbsbewusstein*), or the Freudian ego, but that *it is* as far as *it is* incomplete (Lacan, 2009b). That it is incomplete means that there is something missing, which does not imply that it does not have temporalities. The subject has temporalities, but it does not obey ages. More so, the subject is of the enunciation, that place beyond the declaration. It says more than it thinks it does. If the subject of the unconscious is ageless, but does have temporality, the analytical device aims at the subject in its saying and not at the ego in its alienation in the Other.

We know that doubt demands an answer; however, we will not resort to denying everything that surrounds us. This is the Cartesian proposal. Doubt comes as a consequence of the question about being and the answer is not easy. As we mentioned earlier, the obsessive question is dulled to in "I am or I am not". The premise that implies the subject of the unconscious is: "What am I . . . for the Other? That is the question", that is why the subject is subjected to language inasmuch as it talks (*parlêtre*). The question is about existence, an issue that some would say is philosophical. However, it is placed all the time in the analytical device.

Freud knew how to decant it in his writings, specifically in relation with desire and its negativity. This does not make psychoanalysis an ontology or a hermeneutic, least of all a reduction of Freudian ideas to psychology. On the other side, he resisted to go to philosophy to locate doubting about existence. Instead, he goes to mechanics, physics and biology, which had consequences among his followers, who tried to find the unconscious in the body, thinking it from an inside-outside Euclidian *impasse*.

By proposing models to think an apparatus that has no relation with space as we usually understand it, nor a corporal relation and/or location, Freud inaugurates a scene that states another way to problematize the human. And although he does not elaborate a theory of the instant in which existence is founded, he does leave many clues regarding it. It is Lacan (and not the so-called post-Freudians) who takes up the questions that Freud had asked in order to pose them again.

As we have seen before, talking of the divided subject and its corresponding object as a gap has clinical consequences. By referencing the gap, we mean to say that we think the subject from the perspective of the lack. By lack we understand the absence of the word that could erase the trace that the word itself has left by inscribing as a signifier in the subject. We will then add that if psychoanalysis is interested in the enigmas of sex and death, it is precisely due to them being the two points in which the subject and the *objet petit a* of psychoanalysis fade. The Lacanian aphorism that says "there is no such thing as a sexual relationship" points to the impossibility of an object to complete the subject. Our most intense and complex dramas are ultimately due to this human condition. That is why, in his lecture titled "Discours de clôture des journées sur le psychoses chez l'enfant", Lacan assures the following: "what constitutes the entry in psychoanalysis comes from the difficulty of the being-for-sex. But the exit from it – if we read today's psychoanalysts – would not be more or less than a reform of ethics in which the subject is constituted" (Lacan, 2012).

That there is a difficulty of the being-for-sex means that a mother cannot be completed with an object named child and that the child cannot evolve into a totality either by blocking the mother's lack. Because of that, Lacan talks of a "reform of ethics in which the subject is constituted". But what does this all mean? That given that the object and the subject of psychoanalysis are pierced by the lack, one because it is empty and the other because it is divided, there is no ontology in psychoanalysis.

This way, for Lacan to be able to propose the *objet petit a* as the pivot of his theory, he had to go through the excommunication of the political order (as he called it) and through several arguments with other psychoanalysts, at the time he fed his proposal to other theorists and disciplines. Let us remember that Lacan was a psychiatrist by training and that his arrival to psychoanalysis was due to the social and not to the linguistic.

Lacan through the looking glass

The Lacanian proposal rooted in a clinic of the structure sees its first results with the mirror stage as a device. In it not only do we see the inauguration of the wonderful deception that we know as existence-reality, but also the device in which reality unfolds. To put it differently, the mirror shows the instability of what some say to have in their hands, a reality that fractures at the smallest provocation.

With his final formulation of the mirror stage, in 1949, Lacan not only makes way to a different perspective than that of development, but grants the I (*je*) the symbolic status that was also announced in Freud. However, the scope of Lacan's proposal invites us to think from this point forward on the registers of the symbolic and the imaginary.

In the mirror stage, not only is underlined the importance of the child's capture in the mirror, but also that of the I (*je*) as a function of identifications surfacing from this encounter. The infant is identified with the image in the mirror and under this perspective existence is founded – as its name indicates – outside the infant. The body is presented as other, as the radical otherness to the subject. From there the body is announced as the otherness by being mediated by the Other, it being as language, the means by which the subject will be able to be located in the valley of the egoic mirages.

The I (*moi*) as the specular is in charge of supporting the illusion of think-ing that the I (*moi*) is the subject, just like the Schema L shows. On the other hand, the function of the I (*je*) is that of being the empty pronoun that we go to in order to make the subject's history's symbolic identifications speak. Later on, Lacan will speak of this I (*je*) as the *shifter*, taking Jakobson's theories as a reference.

Why is the mirror stage a (logic) necessity for the human? Why are its effects by far more radical than they appear in animals? Is it by any chance related to the presence of language? These questions are not perilous. They possess the sense to locate the unfinished of the human at birth. The incom-pleteness that lives in the infant by not being able to be independent, not even in his or her bodily movements, delivers him or her as an unfinished being.

> Every psychological and physiological dimension at this Lacanian time appears here with all of its stature. However, there is in all that a luminous "Freudian perception": the place of the lack as a cause. That which oper-ates as a cause is in its structure a failure itself. The mirror stage has the honour of inaugurating the function of the lack as a structuring element in Lacan's work.
>
> (Morales, 2011, p. 105)

Lacan focus his debate in what some theorists are making an effort to rein-force, that is, the I. He underlines it given its function of unknowingness, which excludes it of all that Freud proposed as an ego that is founded on the system of consciousness-perception (Freud, 1923/1986a, p. 27). What we can rescue from that same text is a schematic in which Freud places the ego and the id, the system of perception-consciousness and the pre-conscious in which – as strange as it seems – he places a cap of hearing. It seems that he did not let the importance of the heard word slip as an essential part of the consti-tution of this apparatus. The I (*je*) in its function of unknowingness does not bind the gaze and the image of its body with the Other through the function of the I (*je*), but with the acoustic word that inscribes and serves a support for the infant to identify with what was said by the Other about that image.

We do not consider this a forced reading, because the place of the voice in Lacan has the function of the *objet petit a*, just like the gaze. This acous-tic cap placed by Freud (and not taken up in Lacan) allows thinking of the unfolding of reality, through the function of the mirror stage accompanied by the Other's voice, which has an analogous function to that of the gaze. That is, it does not only capture the child's image in the mirror, but it is also captured by the Other's saying in that same acoustic image. Now, it is not only about the phenomenology of the mirror, because something else happens in that stage. Let us remember that the I (*moi*) is not the subject, but neither is the I (*je*).

For his part, Le Gaufey problematizes the mirror stage bearing in mind that it is not a theory of knowledge. It is not the I confused with the subject who perceives the image in the mirror and identifies with it. Neither is it about the sole perception that is already unified and only received by the subject. Le Gaufey, in his seminar "Les unites imaginaires", says:

> In the case of the perception developed by Lacan in the statute of the mirror, there is a fundamental dimension: the redoubling (*redoublement*). The experience of the mirror was performed with children and monkeys at an age in which the intelligence of both was equivalent. The difference between the ape's experience and the child's before the mirror was that for the ape, the image appeared as another object; while for the child it was precisely that, an image that duplicated an object. Before the mirror, the object does not appear as another object of reality, but reality appears unfolded.
>
> (Morales, 2011, p. 340)

In this stage, the I (*moi*) is alienated from the image that is there. But we already mentioned that it is not just about perception, but about the function of the word that names that image. The image with which the I (*moi*) identifies is not reduced to perception because the subject comes off-centered from the scene and is able to identify that there is a relationship between that I (*moi*) and the object in the mirror. The I (*moi*), on its part, is trapped in that enchantment. That is, the subject wonders about that movement. It is possible to identify this relationship at this level due to the fact that the function of the subject is with the language. The subject cannot be reflected in the mirror, because it is absence.

In this sense, it is not a metaphor when Lacan talks about how the I (*je*) is founded not without a relationship with the image that the Other returns of it. What is interesting is that the identification is not reduced to the image, but to the subject experiencing the effects of the word on that representation. The next step is to clarify that said identification is produced due to something that the mirror does not return. We talk about what cannot be mirrored, like the phallus and the *objet petit a*.

With the intention of analyzing even further the fundamental character the lack has in the construction of psychoanalysis with children, we will next consider the importance of locating the signifier of the lack, that is to say, the phallus (which from Freud to Lacan is a concept that moves from the biologicist metaphors to its logicization).

Phallus: signifier and signification

The function the concept of the phallus has in psychoanalysis leaves no remainder of organicity from what Lacan reintroduces under the premise of the signifier. According to Freud, the first and clearest turn to detach the phallus from its bodily referent, the penis, is described in the following way:

> The main characteristic of this infantile genital organization is its difference from the final genital organization of the adult. This consists in the fact that, for both sexes, only one genital, namely the male one, comes into account. What is present, therefore, is not a primacy of the genitals, but a primacy of the phallus.
>
> (Freud, 1923/1986b, p. 146)

This quote seems obscure at first sight. What we can read in it is the possibility to make a differentiation between the genitals and the phallus, being the latter what differentiates the child's sexuality from the adult's. Both postures are different, even though always in relation to the phallus. Freud proposes as a goal of the adult sexuality that the drives fall under the primacy of genitalia, which does not happen in infantile sexuality, in which the primacy is the phallus.

We also read that Freud's proposal regarding genitality is referencing the goal in a libidinous organization compared to the pre-genital stages of libido in children. However, we observe that Freud draws a child who, through the gaze, is located in a world in which there is no difference, not even between the sexes (that is, before the Oedipus). Likewise, he points out he can only talk from the boys' perspective, being that the girls' is still an enigma. However, it is possible to think that the unknowingness is not only experienced by the boy, since the girl also has her posture before the anatomical difference of the sexes.

What was exposed about the primacy of the phallus in this text is not similar to the proposal Lacan would make years later. The primacy of the phallus references to what some theorists have called the "phallic stage". On his part, Lacan retakes the importance of the phallus in relation to the castration complex, for which the signifier stops having that univocal link with the penis. Freud had already mentioned it with the symbolic equivalence of the boy = father's penis.

It seems like this last equivalence makes more sense with the phallus as a signifier. If the signifier can represent, or well, veil the lack of that word that could say what is missing in language, the phallus would be that signifier that does not say what is missing, but moves through the signifying chain as the signifier of the lack that nests in the Other. This term acquires vital importance in Lacan, especially in the 1958 text "The Signification of the Phallus", in which the phallus leaves aside the direct reference to the penis as an organ to be directly placed in relation to the castration complex, which has a knotting function.

In this sense, Lacan places the castration complex as the element that works as the *ratio* (reason) before which the symptoms will be structured. What is interesting is that for this conception, the phallus has another function, which is to allow the subject to identify with the ideal of its sex.

The subject has a relation to the phallus as a signifier, no matter the sexual position it assumes (Lacan, 2009a, p. 653). Lacan will state something similar in the formulas of sexuation in the seminar *Encore*, in which he goes beyond the theories of gender and, no matter the kind of relationship (man-man, woman-man, woman-woman, etc.) we always play in the position of the phallus as a function.

However, let us go back to the 1950s (Lacan, 1994) when Lacan retakes what he worked in his seminar *The Object Relation*, to problematize the complexity of the girl in front of castration and the phallus. It is interesting the comparison with the Freudian theory that appears in "The Dissolution of the Oedipus Complex" article in which Freud goes to the analogy in the girl, because it seemed dark to him to have access to the girls' clinical material. It is until the text "Female Sexuality" when the difference of that posture is dimensioned and the analogy model stops explaining the woman's position.

This way, it is important to recognize that when Lacan proposes the castration complex as a fundamental part (*ratio*) of the sexes, the discussion he posed – if the penis was envy in itself – loses transcendence. The debate moves into the field of the phallus with the garb of the signifier and its effects, a reformulation that surfaces by dispensing with the model of equivalences between the sexes.

What is interesting here is that the mother is still present as a constituting element both in the boy and the girl, and that the symptoms – according to Lacan – are structured once they know the mother is castrated. According to Rabinovich, this is understood in this way: "That's why the symptom by excellence in infancy at the level of the structure, beyond all the imaginary dimensions that we can give it, is the phobia. Phobias are a sort of failed paternal metaphors, not an 'infantile symptom' originated from a supposed immaturity in children" (Rabinovich, 1995).

This quote directly refers to the function of the castration complex inasmuch as knotting, in the sense of being the *ratio* of the formation of symptoms. And, from what moment is a symptom formed? When knowing that the mother is castrated and therefore, she desires, i.e., when realizing desire exists. There is a subjective operation in which the mother's desire takes a turn of the screw to give way to the paternal metaphor. That is, it is not only about acknowledging the castrated mother, but that in this operation a third element is introduced in order to achieve separation.

So, the symptom as a point of detention (place) in the graph of desire is nothing more than the place in which the signifier starts making sense, therefore, it is not a coincidence that in the graph, s(A) is read as the symptom.

Let us quote Lacan knotting his proposal:

> The phallus can be better understood on the basis of its function here. In Freudian doctrine, the phallus is not a fantasy [. . .]. Nor is it as such an object [. . .]. Still less is it the organ – penis or clitoris – that it symbolizes. [. . .]
>
> For the phallus is a signifier, a signifier whose function, in the intrasubjective economy of analysis, may lift the veil from the function it served in the mysteries. For it is the signifier that is destined to designate meaning effects as a whole, insofar as the signifier conditions them by its presence as signifier.
>
> (Lacan, 2009a, p. 657)

We can see the place in which Lacan places the phallus, that is, far from the genital. A place that puts it closer to Saussure's field of linguistics as well. The phallus is the signifier that is excluded from the signifying chain. It will be a long time before Lacan displaces it from the display cabinet of linguistics and works it as he does here, as a function.

According to what we have mentioned, in his seminar *Encore*, Lacan writes the formulas of sexuation on the board, placing the symbolic phallus as an anchoring point with what he called "The Woman". This localization is not a coincidence, because the other anchoring point was the signifier of the lack in the Other symbolized by S(A) and located in the upper left in the graph of desire. It can then be said that the symbolic phallus has the function of locating the lack in the Other.

The phallus, not being the penis, is placed as a signifier. By the seventies, the phallus was located as a function in relation to the non-complementarity of the sexes. And it is not that the sexes are not linked. Even though it is evident that there cannot be a male without a female, this does not necessarily imply complementarity. Here is the place of the phallus as a logical organizer functioning as the bond without being the amalgam between both sexes. Likewise, it is important to punctuate that the encounter between the bodies does happen. What appears is the complementarity of the positions of the sexuated subject, with which the subject's body can be thought as an otherness, since the subject's body is presented as something that is alien.

What we must rescue is that the phallus as an organizer or function, by being placed as a breaking point between the subject positioned as a man or a woman, will be affected before the Other's demand (whether a man, anatomically speaking, positioned as a woman, or vice-versa). Anatomy has nothing to do in the designation of the must be of each subject, but the position before the Other's demand and the location before the phallus.

In this sense, Lacan inaugurates the gap to think said positions between the *being* and the *having*, terrain where epistemology still tries to locate the object, being that the question does not revolve around it, but before the lack in being of the subject and the lost object, just like the formula of the phantom ($ \$ \lozenge a$) shows. It is not about a subject before an object that completes it, but a subject lacking before an absence.

The child: a subject of the unconscious

With what was problematized earlier, it is clearer that the child does not stop being subjected to language. But what is language? Language is the bridge that the subject has in order to move from one side to the other in a universe that remains undifferentiated, timeless, with no territoriality. With language, the bond that marks the difference in the world is established.

An example will work to locate this. If we are in the city and decide to buy something, the only thing we have to do is exchange money for the object that we intend to obtain. We could make this transaction even in another country, after we exchange our currency for that country's. Now, if we were in a country in which neither the bill's paper or the coin's metal have any value, it would be impossible to obtain anything, for which we would have to create other forms of exchange. Money is worthless if it is not within its own frame of exchange.

In a similar way, language is worthless unless it is within its own exchange system, the Other. The difference with money is that in the world, despite there being thousands of languages, the exchange in signifiers is present all the time. The speaker talks to the receiver "assertively" without passing desire in those signifiers for it. Even in what is related to language it is much more radical, since money is an exchange value in the world, but the signifier, as a support for money, is what opens the real in order to create the world itself. The signifier subverted by psychoanalysis shows that the language is only worth within its own frame, to which the subject is appointed as an absence. The currency for *lalengua* (*lalangue*) cannot go to these "assertive" message exchanges. The signifier does not say what the object and the subject are, it just represents them.

Up until now we can articulate the question: subject of desire? It is not that this question is stated wrongly. The subject, from a phenomenical perspective, is indeed subjected to the Other's desire. Now, the subject and desire are absent in the signifying chain.

Saying "subject of the unconscious" can be another way to call the phantom, because it is in it that the barred subject appears. Facing the absence of the *objet petit a*, both components – barred subject and lost object – have no other function than to sustain desire, whether as impossible (obsession), or as an unsatisfied (hysteria). In the formula of the phantom we can locate the statute of the lack: $, symbolic; *objet petit a*, real; ◊, *losange*, imaginary articulation.

In this sense, subjectivity is depending on elements, like barred subject or lost object, both as a sustain for desire. A desire functioning as face of the lack that articulates psychoanalysis and the subject's saying regardless of age and maturity. These are elements without which it would be impossible to achieve a listening of who talks to us in the analytical device.

As we have seen, the subject for psychoanalysis is not substance, which does not imply that it is not traceable under certain conditions. It is there where Lacan goes to topology, because it is necessary to go to the science that articulates the voids (lacks) not in function of measures, but of relations and places. This new landscape invites us to think the unconscious from a different perspective.

Bibliography

Descartes, R. (2008). *Discurso del método*. México: Porrua.

Freud, S. (1986a). El yo y el ello. *Obras completas Tomo XIX*. Buenos Aires: Amorrortu.

Freud, S. (1986b). La organización genital infantil. *Obras completas Tomo XIX*. Buenos Aires: Amorrortu.

Kojève, A. (1990). *La dialéctica del Amo y el esclavo en Hegel*. Buenos Aires: La Pleyade.

Lacan, J. (2009a). La significación del falo. *Escritos 2* (p. 653). México: Siglo XXI.

Lacan, J. (2009b). Subversión del sujeto y dialéctica del deseo en el inconsciente freudiano. *Escritos 2*. México: Siglo XXI.

Lacan, J. (2012). Alocución sobre las psicosis del niño. *Otros escritos*. Buenos Aires: Paidós.

Morales, H. (2011). *Sujeto del inconsciente. Diseño epistémico*. México: Ediciones de la Noche.

Rabinovich, D. (1995). *Lectura de la significación del falo*. Buenos Aires: Manantial.

Chapter 4

Language in analytical listening with children

Language can name, given that something only appears as such from the moment language names it, but it cannot name itself.

Kafka and the lost doll

As in Paul Auster's short story of Franz Kafka's last year, and under Agamben's look, who argues that " [. . .] to experience necessarily means to re-accede to infancy as history's transcendental place of origin" (Agamben, 1993, p. 53), childhood is presented to us as a supposition of a loss of a certain place understood as the unknown, that does not speak but makes us speak. In this sense, for Agamben, childhood gives way to the word, it is silence and the search for words; the same place of experience and history. So, childhood and language refer to each other, they introduce the possibility to narrate a story to be inscribed in one same filiation line.

On his part, Lyotard proposes:

> Let us baptize it *infantia*, what does not speak, an infancy that is not an age of life and does not pass. It haunts discourse. The latter does not cease to put it aside, it is its separation, but it stubbornly persists thereby in constituting it, as lost. Unknowingly, therefore, it shelters it. It is its reminder. If infancy remains in it, it is because it inhabits in the adult, not in spite of it.
>
> (Lyotard, 1997, p. 13)

For Lyotard, *infantia* translates and searches for the word (that which is not spoken), whereas for Agamben, it is the transcending homeland. Let us place another incidence: *infans*, "the one who does not speak yet". We could say that infancy is the moment in which the subject verbally agrees on language, and that this is the point that we consider a crossroads between the infantile and infancy.

This crossroads weaves the reality of the lost doll that Kafka recovers through discourse, for a girl who makes her reality her lost rag friend. To be more precise, Kafka articulates – through the word – another possibility for that girl, he weaves another story with language, which is not far nor close, it is there, inhabiting discourse. Under these coordinates we can start walking the paths of language that Lacan traces with his "return to Freud".

Freud proposes a new enigmatic journey into the unknown that inhabits the subject through the word. Lacan, following that bet for language's structure, finds that it is in its gaps where the infantile appears, the unconscious; infantile as subjective division that forever announces the distance between structure and development, between subject and child.

To get some clarity between what we understand as infancy and infantile, it is pertinent to retake Esteban Levin's elucidation about these two terms:

> Infancy, doubtlessly, ends, finishes with no return, but the infantile that is instituted there remains in time. However, in childhood, children build memories when playing, which will in the course of time – in the depth of emotions – be imperishable. It is a crouching memory, even in a dim vigil.
>
> (Levin, 2006, p. 12)

Infancy, then, proposes a game with language, placing the expressive condition in a privileged place of absence. Alain Badiou says: "[infancy] as fate and will, as an innovative concept that irrupts from the real to evoke an indefinite time in which memory and remembrance are inscribed in the symbolic order that invites to the imaginary and metaphorical game with its meanings" (Badiou, 2005, p. 99). The bet for infancy is inscribed in attempting against time and its chronology. The polemic is not in the pedagogical consciousness, but in the linguistic posture, in the subjective logic that plays with time and its rhythm.

We consider that the bet on the side of infancy obeys a different way that we will not deal with for the time being. However, we have lightly touched it, because it is time where the subject (child) moves. It is not less important than what we have called the infantile. Although, to continue our road toward the knots and topology, it is necessary to approach more punctually that which the infantile and language implies.

Language and tongue(s): between the infantile and the adult

It is not a coincidence that in Freud language has, as structure, the royal road to pierce the real and from there provide existence to the world. The point we want to border when we talk about the infantile and the adult is different to what Ferenczi suggests regarding these two postures (infantile language and adult language). In "Confusion of Tongues Between the Adult and the Child: The language of tenderness and of passion" (Ferenczi, 1984) he talks about a misunderstanding between the adult and the child, but he locates this misunderstanding in the meaning that each one of the parties gives to it.

The child's language is considered the "language of tenderness" and the adult's, "the language of passion". Both possibilities obey the drive such as Freud evokes it. That is, adulthood is located when drives are unified under the genital drive. In the case of a child, the drives that are still disperse and do not have "reproduction" as an end, or in Freud's words, genitality (Freud, 1986a, p. 167).

We can precise that we will problematize both postures as Scavino suggests, that is, picking up Lacan's formulas of sexuation. Scavino says that the subject of enunciation appears in the masculine position (also called adult), and he places in the feminine aspect the infantile position. To better understand this statement, it is necessary to make an analysis about the influence of anthropology, linguistics and logics in Lacan and his idea of language.

Saussure's and Jakobson's linguistics were the immediate reference for Lacan in that "return to Freud" that started during the fifties. And as curious as it may seem, that contact with linguistics and psychoanalysis itself was enabled by the proximity with Lévi-Strauss's texts. In one of the texts from that time, Lacan says: " [. . .] the life of natural groups that constitute a community is subject to the rules of matrimonial alliance [. . .] Marriage ties are governed by an order of preference whose law concerning kinship names is, like language, imperative for the group in its forms, but unconscious in its structure" (Lacan, 2009c, p. 267).

Lévi-Strauss's influence is evident at that time in Lacan's thought. We can even say that the conception of the unconscious comes to him, in the first place, from the anthropologist. Said unconscious is not the Freudian one. The unconscious presented by Lévi-Strauss works as an unwritten law in culture that binds, which has a direct relationship with the prohibition of incest.

During the forties, Lacan spoke of the symbol and language, however, these still did not have the structuring brand of the subject. His work in this time revolved around the optical models. It was until 1953 when Lacan was able to make the link between law and language and, therefore, with the symbolic. With the development of structural linguistics, the articulation of these three registers began, which twenty years later would force to question the need for topology to be able to account for them in the clinic. Even though by then, the signifier had in its structure that of an unconscious that Freud had located with its own logic. Hence, the Lacanian aphorism in which language becomes the condition of the unconscious. From this perspective, the dimension of language sets aside the conception of transmitting a message from one person to another and reveals itself as that which constitutes reality and humanizes the human being.

On the other hand, structural linguistics include social sciences and kinship rules to locate the subject submerged in the language nets that determine it. In other words, they are signifying coordinates that go beyond the subject and place it in front of the Other even before coming out of the womb.

With this we can move on in our statement. Lacan arrives into psychoanalysis – or psychoanalysis arrives to Lacan, actually – through social sciences, that is, anthropology. Evidently Lacan is not a structuralist; however, the reading that he makes of psychoanalysis is. As an example, we have his Seminar XI, in which he takes a structure of four elements and not just one. This results in the non-partition in Freudian theory. On the other hand, the death drive is a good example of this, because it is a Freudian notion re-thought by Lacan.

The opposition between system (synchrony, axis of simultaneities) and history (diachrony, axis of successions) allows Lacan to observe the logics of language and, with this, rethink the simultaneity of the linguistic signs within a temporal space. The new axis that opens with structuralism also enables looking at the organization without taking the temporal variability into account.

This idea is essential for our work, because it is from Lévi-Strauss and De Saussure where the basis for a reflective thought that mistrusts appearances, qualities and the more evident relationships are established; and the hidden links and significant structures are discovered, which "access the change of direction", establishing a general system.

For this reason, linguistics – the logics of all language – is based on a dual principle, starting from the distinction between tongue and speech in which tongue is the social and codified aspect of language, a universal sign system, and abstract model of varied combinatory possibilities of signs; and speech, an effective, personal, individual and concrete variation of the tongue (or code). In this sense, the particular way to use the tongue is as a group of signs that serves to express an idea. For Lacan, the net of meanings "re-acts historically" upon the net of signifiers, as well as for De Saussure speech re-acts the code of the tongue (Fages and Horne, 1973).

In 1920, in *Beyond the Pleasure Principle* (Freud, 1920/1983, p. 14), Freud describes and interprets a child's game to explain language's inscription. This game consisted in the child disappearing an object while shouting *"Fort!"* (which means "far"), and when making it reappear he would exclaim *"Da!"* ("here it is"). For Freud, said game shows the compulsion for repetition, the recurring need to perform an act that is usually contrary to the subject's desires or consciousness. In this example, the boy, who would desire the permanent presence of his mother, prevents himself against her periodic absences, solving with an object this alternation of her departures and returns.

Before this case, Lacan, on his part, observes in the boy "the determinacy which the human animal receives from the symbolic order" (Lacan, 2009b, p. 61). *Fort-da* presents all the characteristics of a structural alternative: binary opposition articulated in accentuated terms, it signifies and carries out the desired object's absence or presence. The moment in which desire goes through the flesh is also the time in which the child is born for language.

This is important because the subject does something more than control his or her privation. He or she raises his or her desire to the "second power" of language. The action destroys the object that he makes disappear and appear in the anticipating provocation of her absence and her presence. This way, the boy intervenes in the system of the concrete discourse of the environment, reproducing in the *fort-da!* the words that he receives from it (Lacan, 2009d, p. 319). This inscription to language implies the integration of a signifying matter (phonemes, vocals and consonants) offered by the Other. Lacan continues: "Thus the symbol first manifests itself as the killing of the thing, and this death results in the endless perpetuation of the subject's desire" (Lacan, 2009a, p. 319).

On one hand, the signifier (the articulated interjections) is not the Thing (*das Ding*). The fact that the expulsion sign "*fort*" is not the mother signifies the returning "*da*" is of the same order as the first, and is also not the mother. On the other hand, the boy is thrown to the possibility to exercise by himself elements of language that he has received from the Other, and therefore, extend ("perpetuate") the expression of his desire. With this, Lacan enunciates one of the essential propositions of his projects: "If the unconscious can be the object of a kind of reading, [it is because it is] sustained by a structure that is identical to the structure of language. [. . .] The structure of language as it manifests itself in what I will call 'natural languages', those that are effectively spoken by human groups" (Lacan, 2009a, p. 417).

It is true that Freud makes a series of observations on the game of *fort-da*. This *infans*, who could still not articulate signifiers, manages to perform a game that allows him to make a sketch of the symbolic. A sketch of what will later be turned into word, because thanks to the signifier, he makes a presence of an absence. The boy's babbling is an example of the symbolic appearing as a previous operation of agreeing verbally. What Freud intends to highlight in this game is precisely the fact of not reducing the little boy's reel to an object that represents his mother, but reading in it a "piece" of *infans*. Borges says it more clearly: "Time is the substance I am made of. Time is a river which sweeps me along, but I am the river; it is a tiger which destroys me, but I am the tiger; it is a fire which consumes me, but I am the fire. The world, unfortunately, is real; I, unfortunately, am Borges" (Borges, 1980, p. 202).

The reel is not only the signifier but the absence that lies on it. This idea leads us to think on the Freudian thesis about the *Verwerfung*, in which what is rejected (*aussfossen*) implies what is not admitted on the inside, of that which is excluded and reappears on the outside. Lacan, in his Seminar XI, explains it thus:

> If the signifier is truly the first mark of the subject, how can we not recognize in this case – just for the fact that the game is accompanied by one of the first oppositions to be spoken – that in the object to which this opposition is applied in the act, in the reel, in it we must designate the subject. We will name this object Lacanian algebra: the lower case *a*.
>
> (Lacan, 1987, p. 70)

The quote illustrates how, when getting to language, the subject will be dominated by the symbolic order, and also, constituted by it. The subject is knitted by language's *plot*: signifier to significance relationship.

Between 1932 and 1952, the Lacanian posture, influenced by Hegel, was directed toward the imaginary, which is where Lacan accounts for paranoia not being biological, but historical. It is in this way that we find in Freud, beginning with *On Narcissism* (Freud, 1914/1983), elements as function of the unknowingness of the I and the structure of the paranoid knowledge based on envy and mirroring with the Other.

Between 1952 and 1968, during his return to Freud, Lacan worked on the concepts of subject and structure under the influence of Heidegger, Descartes, Lévi-Strauss, De Saussure and Jakobson. During this period he argued that the structure is the network itself where the imaginary world is organized, leaving the real always as a beyond that, by not being able to be turned into a symbol, it becomes a product of the signifier's action.

By privileging the symbolic, Lacan accepted the consequences, which placed linguistics as the discipline for its interlocution. The phoneme and the mytheme, for example, have been the resources used to explain the Saussurean algorithm of significance/signifier, thus constituting the basis for the construction of different formulas, schematics and graphs with which he proposed to guide psychoanalysis toward the formalization.

Likewise, from Lévi-Strauss's and De Saussure's productions, he was able to conceptualize the notion of structure and unconscious. For that, he began with the hypothesis that language is constitutive of culture and that the subject is knitted by language's plot, and approached the conception of an unconscious structured as a language. However, it is convenient to highlight that the sense that Lacan provided to the significance and the signifier is of another order (as opposed to the Saussurian one), due to him installing the supremacy of the signifier. This difference has a fundamental importance in analytical listening. If a patient tells a dream, what is received are chains of signifiers and not significances.

In working with children the same happens, their say in the game makes no sense in the content as it happens in psychotherapy, but the logic rests on the articulation of the discursive elements that oscillate between the words, the silences and their game; that is, their ordered presence. It is in the unconscious that the signifier is what is articulated in a system, that is, in a chain that starts from the first signifier, the phallus. So, Lacan pronounces a decisive answer by establishing the function of the phallus: "The phallus is a signifier [. . .] intended to designate as a whole the effects of the signified, in that the signifier conditions them by its presence as a signifier" (Lacan, 2009f, p. 657).

This reference takes us to the experience in the mirror, in which everything happens at the moment of the relation of the narcissistic identification with the mother. Later on, the father's role is that of a negating word, whose function is to "explain" the mother's absences, making the child be experienced as a "non-phallus" in order to crash against that lack-in-being. But when the Name-of-the-Father is revealed, it is its law the one that signifies that lack-in-being; that is, that the child does not occupy the place of the phallus, that *he* is not the phallus. This does not belong to the world of objects or that of organs, but the symbolic order. The signifier, not being object but absence, designs the lack-in-being, the point in which the child will begin his long and endless search.

It is through this road that Lacan, in his return to Freud, introduced concepts of linguistics, literature, mathematics, topology, philosophy and structural anthropology in an original fashion, adjusting them to the field of psychoanalysis. He likewise approached Freud's ideas, but he did it by extracting the useful knowledge for analytical critique, from the latest advances in other sciences.

It was also in this way that he started conceptualizing the symbolic order as a constituent of the subject, establishing an equivalence to the concept of structure and maintaining that the structure is inseparable from language. Lacan says: "The primordial Law is therefore the Law which, in regulating marriage ties, superimposes the reign of culture over the reign of nature, the latter being subject to the law of mating. The prohibition of incest is merely the subjective pivot" (Lacan, 2009c, p. 268). In other words, the Oedipus complex.

This phrase signals that the Oedipus has been for psychoanalysis the axis around which every subject is organized, being the prohibition of incest its central pivot. The Oedipus complex (Freud) is the phenomenological effect of a structure called the castration complex (Lacan). Through the work of Lévi-Strauss, Lacan read the Oedipus complex to say that in the moment in which a human being is pierced by language and becomes a talking being (Heidegger), there is necessarily a prohibition that institutes the law and social bonds in it.

The prohibition structurally enables exchange and constitutes the social bond. Thus, Lacan related that when law is instituted, desire for the forbidden emerged, not such as content, but as the search for a mythical object to which one renounces in order to find a better one. Whereas the Oedipus complex can be located as fantasy, the castration complex is structural and what gives consistency to the structure is the void, the lack and the impossibility, that is to say, the hole.

This point is nodal, since from 1968 and until 1981, Lacan worked on questions related to the impossible (which had already been worked on by Freud), such as the death drive, the ominous, the navel of the dream, anxiety, and the absence of an object. In the theoretical approach to structure, there is an element added that was always in the shadows, causing effects from there, and being pointed out by Hegel and Heidegger. Said element is death.

From the texts "The Uncanny", "A Child Is Being Beaten" (Freud, 1919/2016) and "Beyond the Pleasure Principle" (Freud 1920/1983), Lacan promoted a movement that goes from the symbolic to the real in his psychoanalytical proposition. He invented new devices, among them, the *objet petit a*, the formulas of sexuation, *lalangue*, the signifier of the lack in the Other and the phantom, not to say the real, but to situate its problems. If the prohibition of incest from the Oedipus is the central aspect for the organization of every structure, its immediate reference is the symbolic castration inasmuch as it allows the inscription of the lack in the unconscious, a term that also refers to the absence-presence (*fort-da*) in Freud.

This idea allows us to consider analysis and specifically the function of the analyst, such as Lacan praises it. The word is the essential dimension in the analytical encounter and, however, the analysis quietens, it emits but an empty word: a word "between". The analyst is first of all that who listens to silences and guarantees, as a witness, the word that the analysand directs to the other. The analyst must not attract the relation of identification itself or make transference of the Oedipus complex on its account. On the contrary, he or she must place the patient in relation to language.

So, in the aphorism "the unconscious is structured like a language", we find two essential doors to be submerged in the Lacanian paths. The first is related to the words "like a", in which Lacan emphasizes the structural condition of the unconscious, because the latter supports its effectiveness as a structure of language. That is, the structure of language is a condition for the unconscious, but in a dimension of the flat space where there is nothing hidden in the deep nor a step into the occult. The Moebius strip is the topological surface that Lacan used to explain how it was that the unconscious only had one face. This means that the signified does not have the consistency that corresponds to a clear or exact reference to the thing that is represented or imagined. The signified remains floating. The set to which it is articulated lacks coherence, because it is related with the net of signifiers. This last governs the group of the significances, whereas the tongue governs the word.

To put it differently, Lacanian psychoanalysis leads to the supremacy of the signifiers.

The second door is where language – which covers the tongue and speech at the same time – has a *languages effect* in its plural use (positive tongue[s]), starting from it only being able to design the structure; plurality as structure, as logic writing (between mathematics and history). Structure whose operation leans on an operator in logical-mathematical terms that enables the change from one position to another. In other words, it is the failure (*objet petit a*) in the structure what allows this change. And it is also the particular way in which language is used, which is not only and precisely the word. Language circulates in other ways besides the word. In children, for example, this peculiar way to use language in plural would be the saying, playing and drawing, which are all supports for language. Lacan insists that the structure of language, as manifested in *positive tongues*, is spoken by the human masses. It is not that there are many languages, but that being a structure, language operates as a support moving past the word itself.

In the seventies, Lacan questions linguistics radically with the objective to grasp the real in language through *lalangue*. That is, from De Saussure's structuralist perspective, including the dimension of the real as an articulation to the word. That is, for the structuralist perspective there is no way to give a place to the failure, the excess, the remainder; that is to say, the enjoyment. There is no place to give to the enjoyment of the drives that is satisfied in the word, in the saying, and that shows that a tongue is a deposit of resources for satisfaction, for which it is naive to conceive language as an instrument for communication that serves exclusive to transmit messages.

As we can see, an epistemic movement is more evident at this moment of Lacan's theory, because we know that enjoyment is forbidden by the act of speaking. But at the same time, there is enjoyment or an attempt to recover enjoyment in the act of speaking itself. It is thus that the concept of language loses lucidity before what Lacan proposes as *lalangue*.

Lalangue: the real in language and enunciation

The tongue is not *lalangue*. Lacan introduces this new term as a consequence of the logical influence on his theories, mainly to the one referring to "there is no such thing as a sexual relationship (proportion)", which does not only underline the disparity between the sexes in relation to the phallus and castration, but the system of universals. From Lacanian psychoanalysis, there is no universal that is not pierced by exception. This logical negative introduces, or rather articulates, the dimension of the symbolic. From there, some other Lacanian negotiations detach that had been worked on previous seminars to

Seminar XIX. . . *or worse*, such as "there is an Other of the Other", and "there is no metalanguage".

To speak about *lalangue* can be read as a *la-langue*, that is to say, singularity, one by one, since there is no universal. But why is it so important to interpellate the universal? The importance lies in the origin of psychoanalysis, the moment in which it is not without importance. It is about the century in which positivism is at its peak and knowledge is thought about as an access to truth, which can be known in its entirety. Or at least that is the idea. The appearance of psychoanalysis emphasizes the failure that positive science has tried to fill up.

The perfect pre-text that Lacan needed to give order to the denial, as a logical element of the structure of language, was provided by Joyce. As we have seen previously the Irish writer disarticulated language and that is where Lacan reads the Joycean intention. The writing of the Lacanian mathemes – clearly not mathematical – appeals to a voiding of signification, introducing them to the game of the equivocal of a *lalangue*.

During the fifties, signification had an essential role. It aimed toward obtaining sense through the movement of resignification. By that moment, signification was located in the imaginary register, which gave it a character of temporality. By the seventies, the analyst did not look to understand or access the meaning; he or she rather needed to find the equivocal, the word play, the voiding of meaning. The repercussions of this clinical posture implicate the subject in its saying, not that the analyst invades it with meaning, or well, its signifiers. The equivocal indicates a new bond.

Lalangue is that tongue that comes from the maternal Other under that singularity that, in spite of being a tongue, has different repercussions in each subject. This way, the bar that separated the signifier from the significance was not only the one that resisted signification through interpretation. Now, that which resists is the border with the Real and at the same time, circumscribes it. The border with the real of language, *lalangue*, is what the patient must deal with, but not without the real presence of the analyst as semblant of the *objet petit a*.

In another aspect, the patient (child or adult) makes a move under transference toward the hysterization of his or her desire. According to the part under the formulas of sexuation, the subject is feminized on the couch, that is, he or she asks about his or her desire. Before this move, there is still a certain subjective disparity. The subject positioned on the male side relates to enjoyment under phallic terms (Ex Φx). On the other hand, the subject positioned in the place of the female has another logic, the logic of *lalangue*, the not-everything. Of all the subjects positioned in relation to Φ, not everything in them goes through this function. There is something in them that happens outside language, because of the inapprehensible of language. In other words: "Man enters the sexual relation *quod castrationem*, that is, as a subject separated from that primordial enjoyment" (Scavino, 2009, p. 254).

Scavino allows us to think of enjoyment as a failed encounter with the real, because every experience of the human is pierced by the difference between the real and its representation, what it denominates, and its discursive figure, the horrific and the pleasant. That is why the discursive construction is an attempt to frame enjoyment through the imaginary staging of the articulation with the signifier. *The real also captures the access to pleasure and satisfaction in its enjoyment.*

Under this perspective, *lalangue* – the real being the group of characteristic equivocals of a tongue that have been accumulated in a history or a writing – carries in itself the effect of the failed search in a language, of the formula of adaptation of the sexes and the failure to find the signifier of the woman that corresponds to the male signifier.

> For Lacan, the, "the woman does not exist" because the article *La* [the] anticipates a totalization, and this universalization is not valid when it is about women. The [*El*] man, on the contrary, exists, only that he should not be that: the man that exists must be excluded, precisely, from human society. There is a male identity, then [. . .]. However, there is not a female identity because the woman does not agree with herself so that there is no exclusion but a split.
>
> (Scavino, 2009, p. 307)

It is in this sense that in the male logic there is a law that is excluded from the legislated domain. The *Urvater* conforms the founder of the universal law that must be anticipated, sacrificed or expelled from itself in order to maintain its consistency. In the female logic, on the other hand, the woman herself represents the exception. The prohibition of the self-reference saves the consistency of the whole, sacrificing completeness.

This idea leads the subject to think in two different ways. The male subject (of the enunciation) that is excluded of the enunciated thesis, and the female (of what is enunciated), which would be the absurd in which any discourse is found from the moment in which it cannot understand itself, being the real a coin with two sides. On one side, the sacrifice that the symbolic demands (loss of the phallic enjoyment) and, on the other, its own impossibility. Language, at the same time as it enables, limits.

This differentiation allows Lacan to take another step in the irruption of the psychoanalytical discourse, that is, from the male perspective, the *saying* is forgotten after what is *said*. For this, *lalangue* is that viscous condition of language. The meaning can change radically, both for a word and a phrase or speech, even for a drawing, a game or any discursive representation.

Toward the end of Lacan's life, the significant structure takes the form of a Borromean knot, thus articulating the three registers: the imaginary, the symbolic and the real. It is in the clinic that this operation has important consequences, that is to say, the subject speaks driven by that desire and suffers the unconscious, since there is a relation between the significant structure and the unconscious desire.

From this proposal, psychoanalysis puts a special interest on interpretation as something similar to an explanation, like a sort of translation that gives a sexual, Oedipal or perverse polymorphous sense to a pain, a complain or a symptom. However, Lacan set things straight by saying that interpretation is not using languages in the way of sense, but it is a game with words, the equivocal and the senselessness.

Interpretation is the way of the signifier as such, liberated from the effects of meaning and the imaginary representation. Interpretation, then, is not comprehended or understood; it is a half-saying that provokes an ambiguity in the subject, a resonance of the equivocal condition of its own saying of the misunderstanding to which it is subjected. By having the experience of knowing more than he or she thinks, the subject (and his or her discourse) revolves around a certain hole of impossibility in *lalangue*.

Now well, if the unconscious is structured as a language and the subject is who suffers the unconscious, then it is not a three-dimensional instance (that is a part of an established apparatus as the Freudian unconscious), but the spatiality of the unconscious is related to the spatiality of the language.

On the other hand, for Lacan, language does not belong to who speaks or who listens, but it is always *being between two*, it is constructed in this interval. The structure of the language is, therefore, two-dimensional, dimensions in which the signifiers are the differential elements, and metaphor with metonymy are laws that put an order so that these signifiers are articulated and moved. It is in this two-dimensionality of the language where the reason resides for which Lacan will make use of grammar, logic, the mathematizing formalization and topology.

So, what function does this plurality of language, the positive tongues or support of language have in the structure? Why can we say that there is an infantile and an adult discursive position? How does it lead us to think analytical work with children and their cure?

If language *is being between two* and is constituted from the relation between two, it implies the split of the subject, division between his or her deepest psychism and conscious discourse. The order of language that is inscribed in the conscious discourse is organized in a separate dimension in virtue of its internal articulations. We do not refer to the reality of the world or the psychism of the speaking subjects, but that it is located between the subject and the real world.

In this order, the subject is represented by several designations like the personal pronoun "I" (*je*), the given name, family indications and so forth. The subject is represented, but it is not present. This split consists precisely in the subject being simultaneously represented by the symbolic order and excluded from it. The split has as a consequence a fading of the subject.

Let us go back to the child. The young boy receives and supports the symbolic order. He is inscribed in it in virtue of a sort of mimicry, but he cannot pretend to dominate it, like in Auster's story, in which the imaginary covers the lack for the doll, symbolizing it (the lack) without confronting it: "The child supports society, its culture, its organization and its language and only has one tragic alternative at his or her disposal: constrain to it or flounder in the sickness" (Rifflet-Lemaire, 1970, p. 129).

This is a way to say that the real shows, but the imaginary and the symbolic insist on veiling it. When the child is born, he or she is named, and with this name he or she receives all the words that submerge him or her in a sea of expectations and projects to tread. But at the same time that these signifiers cover him or her, the child still does not manage to differentiate himself or herself – with the position as son or daughter – from that parental discourse that surrounds him or her. He or she cannot still separate – from the others – those signifiers that will make him or her interrogate himself or herself and, therefore, undertake the fiction of life.

It is in the mirror stage that, on one hand, the coming of a narcissistic unit is constituted, of a kinesthetic subjectivity that allows a first experience to locate the body; and on the other hand, an alignment is determined, a restraint of the child to his or her image, his or her peers, his or her mother's desire. The imaginary is not the symbolic yet. Integrating his or her image to his or her body is decisive for the construction of the subject in the three registers, and this happens from the exchange of looks. Lacan says: "The child turns to that who somehow assists him, though they do nothing more than assist his game" (Lacan, 1988). No one could say something about the imaginary if it was not referred to the symbolic chain.

As we see, it is in the third course of the Oedipal relation, the identification with the father, where the entry to the symbolic order operates, the order of language. The father's main role is that of the word that means law. It is in the Name-of-the-Father where the fundament of the symbolic function is acknowledged, which from the confines of the symbolic time identifies his persona with the figure of law. Likewise, it is essential that the mother recognizes the father as the representative of the law through which the child will be able to recognize the Name-of-the-Father.

If the mother and the child accept the paternal law, the child is identified with the father as the possessor of the phallus. The father again places the phallus in its place as an object desired by the mother, as an object distinct to the child. In this restoration, called "symbolic castration", the father castrates the child differentiating him or her from the phallus and separating him or her of the mother. The child must accept that this castration is signified, entering a constellation in the family triad in order to find his or her fair position. By overcoming the dual relationship with the mother, the child evolves into the subject, therefore, is free from the other two and acquires subjectivity. Thus, the child enters the symbolic world, for which the split is established "between" and the "reverse" of the subject. How does this happen? On one hand, it is in the side of language and social behavior; and on the other, on the side of the I (*moi*) that proliferates through the roles to which the subject submits or is granted; roles that are phantoms, reflections of the real subject that must be searched in its reverse, in the repressed, unconscious part. For Freud, this split is explained through the incompleteness of the conscious discourse, which has some gaps like lapses, wit, forgettings and so forth; discourse that is broken and loses its linear logic to obey the nonsense. This – according to Freud – is even more evident in the dream, which in appearance lacks any sense. The activity of imagination, as well as that of the discourse, penetrate in a veiled and incomprehensible fashion.

To continue thinking about what we have exposed, it is in the clinic where we can see how the child has incidence in the real, but cannot account for it. It is by means of the imaginary and the symbolic that the child discovers the real. From the imaginary are the fantasies, dreams and illusions. From the symbolic, the *fort-da* shows the way through which the child resolves the impossibility.

The child cannot say: "I have understood!", which in Freud's words, would be "making the unconscious, conscious". It is there that it is expected for the subject to be able to consciously confirm a movement in the coordinates of his or her history and where the real appears as a pure impossibility.

The question we want to pose is that the child organizes his or her discourse imaginarizing and symbolizing, but this symbolic chain also has effects on the real, it cannot even assume that which it symbolizes. From there the Lacanaian aphorism: "the unconscious is structured as a language", operation that implies changes in the structure's coordinates. The adult also makes a different movement, that is, desire moves him or her, but leads him or her to assume the lack (symbolic castration).

To say it differently, the child positions itself as a subject before the power of signification (imaginary), agreeing verbally and representing with his or her games and drawings (symbolic), and thus enabling the split from the real (the gap). With this, the child is prey to the unspeakable itself. The real irrupts from the silence with supports for language, or the plurality of tongues, that attempt to occupy this rupture, breaking into the void and constructing new fragments of reality, which only interrogate him or her incessantly about his or her position before the Other, to which he or she can only answer by putting his or her finite being at stake. Likewise, this happens in the real system of the drives – indifferentiated and with no fissures – it can be read only through treading off-centers and transformations that are present in the imaginary construction of the I (*moi*).

The word 'unconscious', says Badiou, designates the group of operations, through which we can access the real of a subject, only in the intimate and imaginary construction of the I (*moi*) (Badiou, 2005). In other words, the real that is opposed to the realm of the image, locates the subject in the field of the being, beyond appearances. For this, the real is victim of an ambiguity.

In short, by approaching the language of the unconscious, psychoanalysis refrains from looking in it for a sort of grammatical syntax or discursive logic. Faithful to Freud, Lacan insisted on interpreting the place of the unconscious through the laws of metaphor and metonymy, synchrony and diachrony, the signifier and its chaining, and *lalangue*, among others.

However, let us go back to language and the *infans*. Agamben says that infancy and language remit to each other, they are played around experience (Agamben, 1993). They both introduce the possibility of the subject to narrate a story to himself or herself, and for that, to be inscribed into a same time of parentage, diachronic and synchronic. As we have seen earlier, from the mirror stage and the Oedipus complex, the psychism of the *infans* will live at the moment of the encounter with the maternal look and voice, and the paternal Law. These are necessary, because they guarantee the psychic life of the subject as a condition of existence. Without them there would not be a subject with a place that was his or her own, even when that place had to be kept building throughout life. Aulagnier writes it thus:

> The mother's flow of words is the bearer and creator of meaning, but that meaning only anticipates the infant's capacity to understand it and to act on it. The mother offers herself as a 'speaking I' or an 'I speak' who places the infant in the situation of receiver of a discourse, whereas it is beyond his capacity to appropriate the meaning of the statement [. . .].
>
> (Aulagnier, 1977, p. 33)

Aulagnier's contributions that articulate the parental place with the social field allow the following reflection: what else if not the word is what grants a place to those who are born, grow as children and must turn into subjects to be inscribed in the world, be children of a history, inhabit the scene of that symbolic world?

It is in this crossroads and this interval constructed between two, who looks and talks (father and mother) and who listens (child), that the phenomenon of language enters the field of the Other. When the speaker's saying goes into the field of the listener (field of the Other) what Lacan calls the "discretional power of the listener" happens. It is there that the speaker is presented with a character of otherness, surprising – himself or herself – of these questions and statements. By going into the field of the Other, it is this Other who throws "what was said" excessively (*objet peti a*). This lower case *a* corresponds to "that" excess (plus), deficit (remainder) or distinct (impossibility), regarding that which we wanted to say voluntarily. This is the character of otherness that allowed Lacan to think that the unconscious is the discourse of the Other. It is from this that Lacan inherits from Jakobson's linguistic studies the categories of "enunciated" and "enunciation", in which the enunciated remits to the *said*, the message designated by communication and which appears in the level of the discourse; and enunciation remits to the *saying*, the act itself of who communicates and that remains hidden or manifests elsewhere.

So, the enunciated will never be taken as such, but as an enigma, hieroglyph in which the subject is veiled. Therefore, when the analyst reads (or listens to) his patient, he or she does it because the equivocal is produced by placing the patient's sayings in writing. What we mean by this is that *that* which is produced in analysis is produced between both positions as a mix so that it is impossible to return to the previous state.

This fact resumes the discussion on the psychoanalytical and psychothera- peutic work, among other disciplines, because they are directed to the work on the symptom and its content, to achieve a displacing and thus fulfill an expec- tation, whereas psychoanalytical work insists on listening and its reading. When the analyst makes semblant of *a*, he or she promotes a change in direc- tion in the patient's saying. It is thus that we find a fundamental differentiation between the I (*moi*) and the subject, that is, the I (*moi*) is always the instance of the imaginary, the place of identifications and alienations. The subject is what emerges at the mercy of the access to language and the configuration of the family of the three characters: the mother, the father and the child. But it can also behave according to the regime of the imaginary, that is, the confu- sion between the I (*moi*) and the subject. The dividing line goes between the true subject and the I (*moi*), that is tricky when it disguises as subject. This is precisely what gives ambiguity of the I (*je*), personal pronoun, whose func- tion is to represent the subject, but which frequently masks it. And the spoken language, by conferring the personal pronoun I an objective statute, culturally accentuates its ambiguity.

From here comes the suspicion that it could be language dominated by the imaginary, by the I (*moi*). The enunciation, on the other hand, is always implicit in the starting point of the symbolic chain. It is here that Lacan introduces a separating bar between Jakobson and the linguists, and modifies the notions of the enunciated, enunciation and shifter (personal pronoun), accentuating the tricky aspects of language and its equivocals. Lacan proposes, then, that for every enunciating fact, the enunciation (the *saying*) remains in a sort of forgetting after the enunciated (the *said*). What does "a sort of forgetting" mean? The enounced coincides with the punctual moment, with the event that something that is said. When we speak and say things, adults frequently forget the act itself of having said them, and we give a greater importance to the content of what is being said (enunciation).

Children, on the contrary, do not accept the forgetting of the *saying* in what is *said*. And for this, the truth does not emerge as an adaptation between the enounced and the state of things, but as the moment of dischord between the *saying* and the *said* (or between signifier and significance), that is, they do not "forget" the act in which it was *said*. Argentinian psychoanalyst Pablo Peusner says it thus: " [. . .] the way in which the child inhabits language is put together from the rejection of the enunciated and the reaffirmation of the enunciation" (Peusner, 2006, p. 35).

In the same enunciating act it is clear that the signifier's primacy, in its differential and systemic character in relation to other signifiers, was an element in this epistemic field that Lacan took again in order to take a step forward in his research; in which he defined the subject for being represented by a signifier for another signifier in a synchronic and diachronic structure at the same time, and allotted another significance to the unconscious according to this logic (linguistics), assuring – as has been said – that "the unconscious is structured as a language".

Starting from the formula "a signifier is what represents the subject for another signifier", Lacan called this signifier a "master-signifier", which represents the subject for another, that is, the master-signifier is the one that founds discourse and at the same time enables the series of all the rest, having a primordial place, that of the agent. This founding particularity is the one that sustains the "total" (or complete) coincidence of the enunciated and the enunciation.

In other words, according to Peusner, the master is a "self-referential" signifier. There, the notion of the unconscious is sustained in a way to interpret a certain phenomenon of common and everyday language. For that, when we say something, we always say more, less or something different to what we wanted to say. And the equivocal that is produced with the "want", tries to tell us something in the sense of a desire of saying.

To better understand this operation in the clinic with children, the symptom, generally detected and recognized by parents or school, provokes a "subjective deafness" by insisting on the repetition, that is, that the saying of the child falls on the child him or herself avoiding the possibility that the analyst – making semblance of the Other – intervenes by asking, punctuating, underlining or playing.

However, the surprise comes when the speaker manages to make this difference between the enunciated and the enunciation; it is the effect of the appearance of the unconscious, the emergence of the question for the desire of the Other; a step of the signifier that founds a want to know of the Other. In this effect in which the unconscious takes a place (Other), the step of the master's discourse to that of the hysteric is indicated.

Milner will call that opening, the gap between the enunciated and the enunciation, "product by homonymy" (Milner, 1999). There, a certain singularity of the position of the child in the structure is inscribed. In this position, the child understands that that he or she is required by the Other, realizing the existence of a desire that moves over him or her and that some practices with him or her are manifestations of desire. However, what the child cannot reach is his or her value as an object regarding that Other's desire: " [. . .] what [the child] expects of the Other-master is to know about what he or she is as an object" (Žižek, 2004, p. 114).

What the child expects of the Other is that he or she is given a certain knowledge of his or her value as *objet petit a*, which will forever remain unfinished. It is thus that in every discourse there is an excessive element, a place that produces remains and a function that prevents the reintegration and the reducibility of these remains.

For example, D. is a young ten-year-old boy who came to my office because he wets his bed. His parents, tired and desperate of this situation, come with the hope that "this" ends. Six months in treatment, the father complains arguing that the boy still wets his bed at night and he often mentions that "in therapy he plays and talks about everything . . . but *that*". However, the father admits that D. has started to ask . . . and saying what he feels and thinks. . . . Which he did not do before, facts that the parents recognize with a certain discomfort, because D. has become "impertinent and rebellious". What is evident is that through these months, the analysis has been the space to talk about any number of things, except – perhaps – to insist about wetting the bed.

With this clinical cut we realize that Lacan did not only think in terms of signifiers, but also in something of the order of the real. This is the main difference with the other discursive approaches, such as Foucault's. So, Lacan is faithful to Freudian discovery: "the unconscious fools us".

Even though the unconscious is structured as a language, it is not the language. There will always be returns of the repressed, formations of the unconscious like jokes, dreams, symptoms, failed acts, which exceed the order of language. It is language that aims to the unconscious, but it is not the unconscious itself. Under this perspective, the lack is located on the level of the signifying structure, that is, there can be a signifier lacking in the speaker.

This empty place is central and will enable the transmutation between the elements. These symbolic elements are not worth by themselves, but by being co-variants, the value of one depends on the rest. With this, the voiding of the reference becomes present, that is, the absence of meaning or total sense. This way, a term does not have a fixed and unique signification in the unconscious, but that this signification will be an effect of structure.

So, language as structure pre-exists the subject, it appropriates him or her. Lacan designates the place of the signifiers: Other. It has already been mentioned that the subject of the unconscious is built in relation to that Other in language that is forever incomplete (eternally barred), because that lack makes the (symbolic) castration itself, allowing the subject to appear as desiring. Žižek says: " [. . .] the hysteric is horrified by being 'reduced to an object', that is, by being invested with the *agalma* that makes him or her the Other's object of desire" (Žižek, 2004, pp. 114–115).

What produces the intolerable effect of castration is not the fact of being deprived of "that", but, on the contrary, possessing it. The castration effect does not begin with a lack, but with a plus or impossibility, idea that escapes the imprint of imagining or thinking that castration is "something" that is not there. Following Žižek, when a subject remains facing a master-signifier, he or she is reduced to an object with a value regarding another, and then, the question for its value in the system of the Other appears. In other words, the subject knows that he or she represents a value regarding the Other's desire, what he or she does not know is what kind of value, whether positive or negative. This knowledge throws him or her to the uncertainty that triggers questions to generate knowledge. Not for nothing Lacan stated the subject's hysterization in his discourse for analysis.

From this reading, we find a definition of the subject that consists in making him or her coincide with the "hysteric subject", in the sense that the hysteric subject is that which is constituted by the question about which is his or her statute, which is his or her value as an object in the Other's desire.

Milner's description of the realm of homonymy is articulated with Žižek's contribution about the master-signifier. This is how it derives in the discourse of the hysteric to inscribe the position of the child in the structure.

Žižek approaches the problems of the construction of the discourse matrix, underlining that every discursive construction is based on the fact of the symbolic *reduplicatio*. That is, the duplication of an entity in "itself" and "the place it occupies in the structure", which refers to a way to classify things from a binary logic that allows differentiating, on one hand, the "self" and, on the other, the place that "self" occupies in the structure. Žižek offers an example by saying that the Pope's place is that of Christ's vicar on Earth, but that it can be occupied by the "self" of a Nazi old man.

As it has been mentioned, if "a signifier is what represents the subject for another signifier", the master-signifier is that signifier that represents the subject for another. Then, that signifier in the place of the master founds the discourse and at the same time, the series of all the rest. That is the charac-teristic to pretend being the place of the agent. However, there is something particular in this master-signifier as an agent, because in that position it is sustaining the enunciated and the enunciation in complete coincidence (self-referential signifier). The notion of unconscious is sustained in a way to inter-pret a certain phenomenon of language, different to the way to use language day-to-day under the discourse of the master.

The infantile and the adult in relation to the enounced and the enunciation

Every time we say something, we say more, less or something different to what we wanted to say. Given that this phenomenon is a regular occurrence, psychoanalysts take a particular position, because we think that what is said as more, less or different, wants to tell us something. The equivocal is produced with the "want", since we consider that it "wants to tell something" in the sense of a desire to say, or also as a text in an unknown tongue.

This phenomenon of language on which we support the definition of uncon-scious equally shows that the discourse that is sustained by the enunciated and the enunciation is never coincident, reason for which the subject is divided when speaking. The illusion of the full coincidence between enunciated and enunciation is sustained from the position of the master-signifier.

However, when the subject manages to make the discursive difference between the enunciated and enunciation, there appear certain effects. The surprise before the effect of the appearance of the unconscious in discourse allows staggering the first signifier (self-referential-master, S_1) in order to slip it toward a second signifier (S_2), thus allowing the subject's hysterization. It is here, as we have mentioned, where the question for the Other's desire arises. Moving from the self-referential signifier to wanting to know about the Other's desire enables posing the question: what do you want to tell me, in what you say, in what I say? Question for the Other's desire.

In the enunciating operation, the logic of the first signifier that organizes the discourse depends on the referent, that is, the signifier does not come first, but appears from its reference. It is because of the second signifier that the first takes its place. According to the place that the elements occupy in the discourse, such will be their implication.

The enunciating function proposes then that the elements or terms do not indicate anything as such. They do not have essence or ontology. Their value depends on the place they occupy in discourse and the relation between these elements. So, a signifier is defined by what it is in relation with other signi-fiers. It has no value in itself, but its value lies in the chaining or relation of difference with the others.

It is worth, then, asking: how can an analyst read the child in order to guide the clinic? Is it about letting desire circulate? Or for a phantom to be consti- tuted? We can ask these questions differently: how does the enunciating act operate in the child? Is *lalangue* a way to enclose or tinge the tongue? Scavino answers the questions as follows:

> The male subject [adult position] truly founds his own position on author- ity. But because of this he cannot get rid of the inherent transgression [. . .]. In the female aspect, (infantile position), on the other hand, where there is no meta-language, truth appears as discord between the saying and what is said. And hearing this discord is the psychoanalyst's task.
>
> (Scavino, 2009, p. 309)

The subject of the enunciation, the male subject or the adult position is a self- referential founding exception. In this sense, the discourse is above all the possi- bility of everything, an unfounded fundament. But at the same time, the female answer, the subject of what is enunciated or the infantile posture, is the aporia or *impasse* in which any discourse is found at the moment it cannot, without incur- ring in a paradox, understand itself. We could dare say that the male or adult solution is the way to avoid the *impasse* of the unspeakable female or infantile. That is, the subject of the enunciation or the unconscious does not believe in his or her own death.

From child to subject: about sexuation and the phantom

A six-year-old boy was drawing something very similar to a landscape with- out achieving any sort of order in the distribution of the elements. In the disar- ray, a tree was located on top of his house and a bicycle. His mother, worried, asked him: "but . . . is that bicycle flying?" The little boy, without worrying too much, answered: "the thing is, it's a dream".

Coming to this point and resting on the Freudian proposition, we could think that there is a phantom in the child that is tied to the Other's desire, which surfaces with the access to puberty. However, for Lacan, the child's discourse in the analytical space is just like any other.

If we follow Freud's first argument, and if we take it in terms of sexuality and not sexuation, it is inevitable to say that the *Urverdrangung* (primary repression) is finished being built with the access to puberty. That is to say, the drive, being partial, is completed with genitality, producing sexuation as an effect, *après coup* of any previous scene. However, if we go to the Lacanian definition, the phantom is the structure of the subject itself. It is the signifi- cant arrangement with which a split subject tries to "catch" that object that escapes, but constitutes him or her: the *objet petit a*. This phantom is one of the only possible mediators in the relationship with the Other and between the registers.

In Lacan's work, this mediation is viable thanks to the existence of a logic whose description starts from a definition of the alienation and separation movement, which has as a consequence the staging of two fundamental statements like "there is no universe of the discourse" and "there is no such thing as a sexual relation".

From this perspective it is possible to locate achievements to localize the concept. In the first place, we situate the description of the alienation-separation axis as conducive to the act of subjective foundation. By this means the signifier goes to represent a subject for another signifier according to the corollary of production of the reminder, a *plus* or impossibility named *objet petit a*. Alienation and separation are the two fundamental operations to formulate the subject causation. Both are ordered in a circular and non-reciprocal relationship, which means that there cannot be one without the other, because each one leads to the other. Besides, they are not reciprocal since they are different, that is, each one functions according to a determinate logic, which is different for each case. There cannot be alienation without separation or vice-versa. In this, Lacan is fairly explicit: "[. . .] no relationship is conceivable that engenders alienation apart from the relationship with the signifier" (Lacan, 2009e, p. 799).

This assumption points to the subject being alienated from the Other and must be separated from the Other. However, the first operation, which is the alienation, is to the signifier and not the Other. The signifier produces alienation, because there is no signifier that represents the subject by itself. Lacan says: "The register of the signifier is instituted on the basis of the fact that a signifier represents a subject to another signifier. This is the structure of all unconscious formations: dreams, slips of the tongue, and witticisms. The same structure explains the subject's original division" (Lacan, 2009e, p. 799).

In second place we locate writing in this founding act described as *Urverdrangung*, under the way of the denominated the discourse of the master and, in the third, we find the affirmation that points that, in origin, *lalangue* spins in circles, in a constant *ritornello*, thus producing a flow in sense that unavoidably has to be fenced or relieved by the tongue. The source that fences that flow is the master-signifier, any given signifier that becomes, from that act of subjective constitution, in the only support to access a tongue. This is a tongue in particular, of which if the master-signifier is the support, the Other is the guarantor.

Before this panorama, the formulation of the act of subjective constitution supposes a logic of the phantom that allows highlighting some questions. First, there is no more trace in the subject than the representation by a signifier, operation that is called *Vorstellung-Repräsentanz*, which is nothing more than the split itself. Second, there is only the *Dasein* of an object that by definition slips away. Well then, to this split subject corresponds a lost object, which never existed in the first place. It is a void (*objet petit a*) that produces the illusion of an object that could be found and thus complete the subject in lacking; third, what was stated previously is only viable in concordance with the foundation, through the act of that which is called subject of the enunciation. According to what was already exposed, the *je*, subject of the enunciation, is not the *moi*. The subject is categorically divided between enunciation and the enunciated, because there is no enunciation without phantom.

It is important to emphasize that Lacan took up the concept of enunciation from Benveniste. For this linguist, the enunciation is the only possible generator of the enunciated, that is, it is the act of appropriation of the tongue before the enunciation. For that, the tongue is carried out in a discourse that supposes to locate the presence of the Other. In other words, the tongue exists as possible only when the *infans* has been exposed to the possibility of the language.

From what has been stated, it is interesting to think about the enunciation in the child. Let us take as an example the following experience: Let us imagine a form that a child brings home from school and asks his father to sign it. The document says: "I _____ authorize my son to participate in the football tournament. . . .". The boy, to make the work easier for his father, completes the form with his father's name and only asks him to sign it.

It is evident that there are at least three people involved in this operation, the boy who wrote the father's name, the father who signs the document and someone who wrote the form. So, what is the point of interest? Is it about seeing who the empirical author of the enunciation is? What is of interest is to know who the author of the enunciation is. It therefore consists in that position that is locatable in the place of the *je* as an anchoring point, that is, in the polyphonic multiplicity. Is it possible to think of an enunciation that is not held on the side of the Other? When a child says something that we know was said by the parents or teachers, who is the author of the enunciation?

There need only be a separation, because it is about what Lacan rescues from Freud when the boy (who would later be the "Rat Man"), fed up with his father, because he had displeased him, says: "hey you, lamp, plate, napkin!" These are the words that the boy has to insult.

With this we mean to say that any signifiers are necessarily ordered in such a way by the primordial signifier – question of the sexuation – in order for the act of appropriation of the tongue to be produced, that is to say, the enunciation. Act for which the subject becomes an agent of the discourse in a place of enunciation that is not, and cannot be, without a phantom.

To finish, we once more reiterate on what we have mentioned: that the object is empty and the subject split means that there is no possibility to name death or sex. There is no signifier that represents the Other's sex and death. The famous Lacanian aphorism that says, "there is no such thing as a sexual relationship" is what points the impossibility of an object to complete the subject.

That there is a difficulty of the being-for-sex means that a mother cannot be completed with an object called "child", but the child cannot become a totality by capping his or her mother's lack. And, however, the attempts for this to happen exist, and for that Lacan talks of a "reform of the ethics in which the subject is constituted". What does this all mean? That given that the object and the subject of psychoanalysis are failed, one because it is empty and the other because it is divided, there is no ontology in psychoanalysis.

There is no structure of the being in psychoanalysis, but an ethics of the constitution of the subject. In psychoanalysis there is no definitive way of being, but ethical positions before a lack in being. For this, there is not an analyst being, but a position that is assumed in the structure, not ontologically, but in an ethics of listening, as that of reading the child,[1] so that some previously unnoticed possibilities could emerge. Lacan says: "The phantom in which the subject is captive, and which as such is the support of what is expressly called the reality principle in Freudian theory" (Lacan, 1975, p. 75).

Bringing up ethics has its complications, in that it points to a universal well-being, and that, as we have seen, the notion of universal in psychoanalysis cannot be included without the not-all. To end this chapter, we will only suggest the analyst positioned in relation to ethics, which includes the death drive. That is to say, the appearance of ethics is seen for its effects and that same instant is in which the analyst intervenes in act under the listening of that which the patient says.

Note

1 The child can take a position in the structure as a symptom, imaginary phallus, symbolic phallus or as a specter.

Bibliography

Agamben, G. (1993). *Infancy and History*. London: Verso.
Aulagnier, P. (1977). *The Violence of Interpretation*. East Sussex: Brunner-Routledge.
Auster, P. and Gómez Ibáñez, B. (2007). *Brooklyn Follies*. Barcelona: Editorial Anagrama.
Badiou, A. (2005). *El Siglo*. Buenos Aires: Manantial.
Borges, J. (1980). La nueva refutación del tiempo. *Prosa Completa 2*. Barcelona: Bruguera.
Fages, J. and Horne, M. (1973). *Para Comprender a Lacan* (1st ed.). Buenos Aires: Amorrortu.
Ferenczi, S. (1984). Confusión de lengua entre los adultos y el niño. In S. Ferenczi, *Obras completas Tomo IV*. Madrid: Espasa-Calpe.
Freud, S. (1914/1983). Introducción al narcisismo. *Obras completas Tomo XIV*. Amorrortu editores: Buenos Aires.

Freud, S. (1919/2016). *Obras completas Tomo XVII*. Buenos Aires: Amorrortu editores.

Freud, S. (1920/1983). Más allá del principio del placer. *Obras completas Tomo XVIII*. Amorrortu editores: Buenos Aires.

Freud, S. (1986a). Tres ensayos de una teoría sexual. *Obras completas Tomo VII*. Buenos Aires: Amorrortu.

Freud, S. (1986b). Totem y tabú. *Obras completas Tomo XII*. Buenos Aires: Amorrortu.

Freud, S. (1986c). El malestar en la cultura. *Obras completas Tomo XIII*. Buenos Aires: Amorrortu.

Lacan, J. (1975). *El Seminario de Jacques Lacan 20*. Buenos Aires: Paidós.

Lacan, J. (1987). *El Seminario de Jacques Lacan 11*. Buenos Aires: Paidós.

Lacan, J. (2009a). Psicoanálisis y su enseñanza. *Escritos*. México: Siglo XXI.

Lacan, J. (2009b). El seminario sobre la carta robada. *Escritos*. México: Siglo XXI.

Lacan, J. (2009c). Función y campo de la palabra y del lenguaje en psicoanálisis. *Escritos 1*. México: Siglo XXI.

Lacan, J. (2009d). Variantes de la cura-tipo. *Escritos 1*. México: Siglo XXI.

Lacan, J. (2009e). La posición del inconsciente. *Escritos 2*. México: Siglo XXI.

Lacan, J. (2009f). La significación del falo. *Escritos 2*. México: Siglo XXI.

Lacan, J (1988). *Dos notas sobre el niño*. Buenos Aires: Manantial.

Levin, E. (2006). *¿Hacia una infancia virtual?* Buenos Aires: Nueva Visión.

Lyotard, J. (1997). *Mainmise*. Buenos Aires: Eudeba.

Milner, J. (1999). *Los nombres indistintos*. Buenos Aires: Manantial.

Peusner, P. (2006). *Fundamentos de la clínica psicoanalítica lacaniana con niño*. Argentina: Letra Viva.

Rifflet-Lemaire. A. (1970). *Jacques Lacan*. Bruxelles: C. Dessart.

Scavino, D. (2009). *El señor, el amante y el poeta*. Buenos Aires: Eterna cadencia editorial.

Žižek, S. (2004). *Violencia en acto*. Buenos Aires: Paidós.

Chapter 5

Toward a topological articulation with the clinical praxis

Of the real there is a vague idea via reason, the signifier doesn't achieve to embrace it. The real is presented to us as an eternal repetition, nevertheless, as speakers we don't have more tools than language to say it. In other words, to make hole in the real to border it and with this, to make, to know how to make.

The end of the analysis doesn't imply emptying the unconscious

From where and with what elements can the end of the analysis of a child be posed, if this doesn't necessarily finish with the cession of the symptoms? "From where", as we posed it at the beginning, would be the field invented by Freud, that is, the psychoanalysis, which implies the dimension of the unconscious and the infantile. As we know, it is not about finding it inside or below of something (as some call it, subconscious), but in the inside-outside. With this, by not noticing the new element, the logic of the internal-external falls short and it is in that sense that we must turn to topology.

Lacan's use to topological elements is not exclusively at the end of his teaching, as is considered sometimes. Even in "The Function and Field of Speech and Language in Psychoanalysis", written of 1953, Lacan shows already the importance of this tool.

> To say that this mortal meaning reveals in speech a center that is outside of language is more than a metaphor – it manifests structure. This structure differs from spatialization of the circumference or sphere with which some people like to schematize the limits of the living and its environment: it corresponds rather to the relational group that symbolic logic designates topologically as a ring.
>
> If I wanted to give an intuitive representation of it, it seems that I would have to resort not to the two-dimensionality of a zone, but rather to the

three-dimensional forms of a torus, insofar as a torus' peripheral exteriority and central exteriority constitute but one single region.

(Lacan, 2009a, pp. 307–308)

Although for this moment Lacan proposes the word as the means with which the subject can solve a certain end of the analysis, it is important to observe the call to a non-intuitive spatialization. That is, a different separation to an "inside-outside" to be able to locate the unconscious.

Concerning the second part of the question, that which refers to the elements that we can use to articulate our proposal, let us say we will take them from the Lacanian topology. From there, it can be read the saying of the subject in his logic temporality, as Flesler points out well (Flesler, 2007).

The question about the end of the analysis, or about the purpose of a child analysis and in what terms conclusion of it can be considered, is not a closed topic. Before our question related with the possibility of thinking an end of analysis, we can pose "an end" not as something terminated, but as a change of subjective position, since once the subject of the unconscious is listened, by the presence of the analyst desire, one cannot go back to the previous state.

In Freud, we find an end of analysis in terms of assumption of the castration, or in other words, the meeting with the living rock of it. Lacan, as we have seen, talks about more than one end to an analysis, none of which aims to an ideal as an expected goal. On the other hand, in the clinic, frequently, these theoretical endings do not necessarily correspond with the ones we live in the therapy office. If we thought of a cure aiming to an ideal, we would be describing a person that "is happy" now with his job, with the things he possesses, someone who will not relapse in neurosis. On the contrary, if we talked of a child whose obsessive symptoms have stressed, we could think of a fail treatment, because this does not appear as the ideal ending of the psychotherapy. To elaborate on this, let us take a look at a clinical case.

Joaquín or the so-called *mal*-function

My first approach to Joaquín was through his mother. In the first interview with her, the figure of Joaquín began to configure. Introvert child, isolated, with a marked inability to express what he wants, feels or needs. Both her and her husband – she told me – have decided on "therapy" for him as a result of the neurologist diagnosis.

– Joaquín suffers from Attention Deficit Disorder along with certain immaturity in the psychomotor development and some little troubles to express himself – the mother said in a provocative tone, as if she wanted to unveil that during that time she was studying psychology. It did not take her long to bring it up, including the comment about the recognition her husband enjoyed in the architectural circle of Mexico.

– You know? – continued the mother –. I want to have my own therapy office as soon as possible, but . . . my husband is very busy with his own things and if my children already spend so much time by themselves, imagine now that I. . .

The next week I met Joaquín. At that time, he was still a child, his gaze reflected the ten years he had lived. From that moment and for almost six months, Joaquín was silent. It was as if his words were unfolded in his corporeality. Through gestures and certain representations with the toys of the office, he established some sort of communication due to which, along with the punctuality of the child, which surprised me every session, I bet for the transference that little by little was being built. The mutism threshold began to crack when Joaquín started to comment on small anecdotes of the school and of his brothers. He told me he is the oldest of four brothers, one brother is two years younger, and the two youngest, who are non-identical twins, five years younger than him. When he told me those stories, both his behavior and his speech fluctuated between the demand for help and the apathy. It seemed like he, in a certain way, was resigned to his condition and had nothing else to talk about besides what the neurologist had diagnosed. "It was all said". A year and a half passed and Joaquín continued to be punctual in his sessions.

We suspended the analysis for two months, since his family had the custom of spending every summer in his maternal grandparents' house, in California.

During that summer, Joaquín has turned twelve years old. My idea that he was enjoying his vacations blurred when one afternoon, when I was at home, I received a call.

– Hello – I answered.
– Hello Liora, I want to talk to you – it was him.
– Go on Joaquín, I'm listening – I exclaimed in a friendly way. I received as an answer an overwhelming silence that didn't presage anything positive.
– Go on Joaquín, I'm listening – I insisted with no intention of pushing him.
– I don't know what's going on with me . . . I cannot tell you . . . – he murmured –. Almost with no voice, he said goodbye, and I had no choice but to do the same.

During that summer I received around forty calls similar to the first one. It is needless to say they were all impregnated of a strange atmosphere, where the voice of Joaquín made me think that something really painful was happening to him and that it was complicated to express it. The intense desire of telling me "something" about what happened was more than critical, such as the express need of me being there with him, in California, to listen to him. This fact confirmed that, although a little more than two years of work have passed, in that moment the transference was concretized.

When he came back we continued the sessions. For a couple of months Joaquín once again wrapped himself into his silent stronghold. Understanding his discomfort, I let the silence continue. Finally, one day, with a distressing tone, he said:

> – I need to talk about this, because if I don't do it, these obsessions will never go . . .

In that moment, the word "obsessions" was installed in my head causing an echo that seemed endless. Every resonance emitted the same question: what kind of obsessions is he referring to? Without showing the intrigue that the word caused in me, I followed the conversation course simulating that this type of exchange has always existed. The fact that Joaquín had said "something" that referred directly to his pain revolutionized the analysis. From that session, his words freed his fears.

> – During this summer that I was in my grandparents' house something terrible happened to me. I was on my grandmother's computer and when I turned it on, a pornographic website appeared. It was a virus. Curiosity caught me and I opened the website, and . . . I saw . . . horrible things . . . – said Joaquín not being able to conceal his pain.
> – What did you see? – I asked.

In that moment, there was silence. The face of Joaquín exhibited a lachrymose gesture. As an answer, the most accurate was his crying.

During the next session, Joaquín brought his pain to the table. He seemed decided to talk about it:

> – The website I saw was hideous – he said as if he wanted to justify his pain.

I kept myself in silence waiting for him to talk more. Joaquín's lips rhythmically ondulated as if he was freezing:

> – Like men with children – he muttered.

With emerging tears at the edge of his eyes, again the crying began as expected.

During two more sessions he delved into the issue. What was the most interesting for me of all the things exposed by Joaquín was the exacerbated anguish he felt when he couldn't turn off the machine or change the website, up to the point of breaking its cable with the intention of breaking the computer down. As if he wanted to erase up to the minute detail of the images that caused him so much terror. However, the responsibility of the malfunction was still his, so he went out to look for an antivirus to "fix" the machine, which he never manages to do.

The "broken down" computer was for Joaquín a more than convincing reason for never coming back to his grandparents' house. With a laconic "no", Joaquín stopped the insistent proposals of his mother to go back there. When his parents realized this, they supposed that "something" had bothered their son during his last visit, but they never managed to know what it was.

The analysis continued its course. During the next sessions Joaquín tried to evade the issue arguing he did not want to talk of "that" topic, a decision that I respected. However, he always came back to it of his own will. He used to tell me if he talked about "it", he was sure he would be able to overcome it.

From the time Joaquín turned thirteen years old, our relationship was already solidified. However, it was evident that building relationships with other people was highly complex for him. During the breaks at his school he was always alone. He felt his conversations were "dumb and shallow", and the girls didn't lay eyes on him. All this imprinted in him a crestfallen air to his person. During this period, Joaquín's life revolved around an environment not at all flattering. When his father lost his work for legal reasons, the marriage began to break, partly due to the economic imbalance. During an aggressive discussion between his parents, which Joaquín listened to from his room, he found out his mother had had an extramarital relationship. This was beyond him, it provoked in him a great disappointment, anger and despair toward her. It also stressed the detachment from his father. This maelstrom brought with it the imminent divorce of his parents.

> – It disgusts me to know that I was born from her, that I was in her body – he strongly disapproved of his mother.

It was not just the infidelity act that caused him anger, but he was also upset because she didn't exercise her profession:

> – I don't understand why my mother doesn't work, she doesn't do anything during the whole day. . . . Why if she studied psychology, she doesn't have a therapy office like yours?

With his parents definitely separated, Joaquín and his brothers stayed to live with their father, while the mother traveled frequently to California. During this period Joaquín's attitude in the sessions was really thorough, so to speak. His behaviors and obsessive ideas, that revolved around his "condition", as he used to call it, tried to clarify the reason of it. Through notes he carried to sessions where he wrote the topics he wanted to deal with he conditioned himself not to lose sight of anything. It was imperative his need to build an answer. During the sessions, Joaquín's speech was situated in the rational, while under the skirts of his words the affective was hidden. Along this stage of analysis, Joaquín decided to stop taking his medication. Words seemed to boost him to believe in them and to realize that through them things could happen. However, his rash decision of nullifying his medication resulted in an imbalance, which made him feel autonomous to his own body. I remember he once commented:

– I feel as if my body was one and I am another. My body goes faster than what I think.

I still wonder what had he seen on the computer that summer. What was that of men with children? Without a doubt, that ominous vision displaced him, dis-centered his life, configuring a distressing topic inside his speech.

The clock struck five in the afternoon, just the agreed hour with Joaquín for his appointments. Since my four o'clock patient had not attended, I was attentive to the sounds that came from the waiting room. I heard someone entering the bathroom, the toilet didn't activate, I did not hear a sound that exposed its use either, just the faucet of the sink and the strong water stream that indicated that someone, most probably Joaquín, was in there. An energetic hand rubbing caused me some curiosity. If it is him, why is he washing his hands so frenetically? I wondered. My suppositions were not wrong, because just after the noise in the bathroom ceased I listened to a door opening, then closing, some steps, and after that a knock at my door, which I answered with "come in". It was Joaquín. When he entered, I realized he was holding the door knob protecting his hand with a disposable tissue. I dissimulated.

– How are you? – I said.

Joaquín stayed a moment in silence, he sighed slowly and said:

– I don't like to commute using public transportation, people are dirty.
– Dirty? – I answered
– Dirty – he answered firmly – Yes, people grab public objects after having sexual intercourse or masturbating and they don't wash their hands.

– Dirty as the door knob?

When he understood I had seen him, Joaquín was speechless. Seconds later he reacted and said:

– Lately, I usually do it. I also wash my hands very often – he made a pause
    –. Mmm . . . last weekend I went to eat with my family to a restaurant,
    I asked for a fish in white sauce and when the waiter arrived and put the
    dish in front of me, I imagined that the sauce was sperm. It made me
    feel really sick.

In subsequent sessions, his speech concatenated even more with the incident of that summer. He told me that the sensation of disgust persisted to such a degree that the discomfort was the value to determine if a day was good or bad. Good days were those when he could get rid of the sickening memory of the house of his grandparents, while the bad ones were linked to "dirty" activities like masturbating and watching pornographic videos. Despite the disgust and the pain that these actions produced in him, he had to deal with them to obtain pleasure. Under this context, bad days were days of ambivalent emotions.

At seventeen years of age and studying his senior year in high school, Joaquín meandered through his doubts, which paralyzed him. However, after finishing his studies he went to France where he worked for some time as a waiter. The fact he had chosen that work seemed to me a favorable event for his development, considering his obsessions with people. He never broke communication with me.

Back in Mexico we resumed the analysis. Joaquín had already resolved to study architecture, however, the tightrope was again under his feet, consequently changing his mind to study psychology two days before the start of school. Considering his father is an architect and his mother is a psychologist, his choice was meaningful. Even so his stability – in a certain way – was relative, since he decided to continue his career in California and not in Mexico. Joaquín, through a lot of effort, achieved to get a scholarship, an achievement that seemed to me a more than deserved triumph. Just when he was about to go, doubts paralyzed him again and he commented to me that the best thing – he thought – would be to stay in Mexico. I drastically intervened making him understand he couldn't lose an opportunity like this. Besides, it was a good moment to make a movement in the analysis, therefore we concluded. In that moment, the eyes I have known ten years ago were filled with tears. Joaquín told me I was very much important in his life and that he thanked me for everything I have done for him.

After a couple of weeks, his voice filtered through the auricular of my telephone. This mode of communication assured him once again that I would be there – as long as he found his answers – to listen to him. He commented his roommates persisted in creating an unbearable atmosphere in the room through sick jokes of a sexual character and other attitudes of young men of his own age. My comments were suggestions for him to let things go with his roommates.

The telephone stopped ringing. From time to time I get calls from him. Every time Joaquín comes to Mexico he visits me. His doubts still live in him without affecting his projects. He has never resumed the incident that marked him so much. The computer he "broke down" that summer is that dim chapter of that novel that we abandoned and that awaits to be completed. Just like the abandoned chapter, the malfunction of that machine demands a "fixing" that can be done in the hands of the applicant. "A fixing" that, for Joaquín, is still pending.

Three months ago, I received an e-mail in which Joaquín, as head of the Student Council of Psychology of his university, invited me to impart a conference on Lacanian psychoanalysis. Maybe this is a call to readjust that computer and end this way the gloomiest chapter of his own novel? Will this be the completion of an analysis or a new beginning?

Last year, on November 6, I received a call from Joaquín. All his concerns – he emphasized – revolved around the stress he had been living as a consequence of his position as head of the Student Council of Psychology, his two jobs and the inconveniences that his social isolation generated in him. However, I guess the main cause for the call was the fact of having to spend Thanksgiving Day in the house of his grandparents. His distress for going back there was evident. He asked for advice on how to face the fact, by the same time he commented he had left his bottle of Rivotril in Mexico, and that without it, he didn't think he could circumvent the situation.

The telephone rang. It was Joaquín again. It had been twenty days since the last call we had.

– It was all very calm – he emphasized happily. It surprises me that I feel so good. You know? I didn't have unpleasant memories and I felt comfortable in the grandparents' house. What is this about, Liora?

I kept silence and waited for his reaction.

– I have certainly been working a lot for this moment.

After he finished his statement, the line was left in silence, until he asked:

– Do you have time now?
– Time for what? – I answered.
– I just want to tell you something that has made me uncomfortable lately.

– Sure Joaquín, tell me.

– Some weeks ago I went to see a psychologist of the university, and between the things I commented to her, there was a memory of my child-hood. When I was ten I went to the doctor so he could check my hernias. The physician told me to pull my pants down and he checked me behind the genitalia. When I finished telling that, the psychologist immediately said "that was not normal". I don't know why the psychologist said this. From that moment I haven't been well, I have even thought if the doctor really made me something.

– And what do you think of it? – I asked so he continued and talked more about it.

– I don't feel that doctor molested me, but since the psychologist told me that, the memory produces in me something strange. Besides, every-thing that has to do with sex still reminds me of what happened in the house of my grandparents.

The last time Joaquín came back to México he came to see me. We talked...

– I wonder – he said with a thoughtful tone, why didn't my parents talk to me about that?

– About what, Joaquín? – I answered.

– When I was around ten or eleven years old, I don't remember quite well, I asked them things . . . concerns about sexuality. I remember that caused me a lot of embarrassment, but I needed them to talk with me about it! – he strongly emphasized, as if he wanted to yell it – And do you know what they did?

I simply remained quiet and nodded at him to continue.

– They bought me books and videos so that, according to them, I was informed. Liora, why did they buy those things to inform me? I didn't want information, I wanted to listen to them! I wanted them to talk to me about it!

The call that Joaquín did to his parents was answered by an intermediary, books and videos that are bought in any bookstore, with any credit card, at any time. Instead of talking to Joaquín, his parents preferred to buy him informa-tion, to buy (his) silence.

From the living body to the signifier

To pose a reading on the current case we pretend to schematize it by times, not necessarily chronological. With this we will try to tighten diverse lines that are woven in the analysis, that is, imaginary, symbolic and real, besides the positions that the subject occupies regarding his story and the treatment. The proposed times are the following: (1) ". . . good days, bad days", the moment when Joaquín breaks the silence. (2) "I had to break it down", moment of the *tyché*, of the eruption of the traumatic real of the Thing, that is the core itself of the situation. The real of sexuality is presented to him in the maternal grand-parents' house. Joaquín is not passive before this meeting and does not cease either looking for the Thing, which announces the traumatic of sexuality. (3) "Memory of age ten", moment in which the subject receives the message in an inverted way and in which, despite not being on the couch nor attending two or three times a week, as an orthodox analysis would point out, the demand of the subject is still held by different paths. Such paths, that in the beginning of psychoanalysis were the correspondence, are now supplemented by technol-ogy, the same that points out to an unfolding, to a cybernetic virtual reality.

... Good days, bad days

After six years of analysis, Joaquín achieved a subjective movement. It was quite interesting to listen to how he expressed his ideas. Sometimes, he brought written on a paper the topics he wanted to address during the session, with the intention of not letting go of any important point and of not being distracted with any other aspect.

For this moment of the clinical work, Joaquín decided by his own convic-tion to go off his medication. However, it was not easy for him since there were days in which he used to say he felt like he was "unsettled", with "strange sensations in the body". He commented: "I feel as if my body was one and I am another. My body goes faster than what I think".

When he entered and left the therapy office he had to go to the bathroom to wash his hands. He took a disposable tissue to open the door. He couldn't stand doing it directly with his hand. One reason he didn't want to go far to a university was that he had to commute using public transportation, a situation that meant he had to mix with "dirty people". On one occasion he commented that people touch public objects after having sexual intercourse or masturbat-ing and they don't wash their hands. He once went to a restaurant to eat with his family, they served him a fish bathed in a white sauce and he imagined it was sperm, which made him feel sick.

He insistently said he had "good" days and "bad" days. The "bad" ones were directly related with the incident that summer. He used to wear the clothes he took to that vacation to come to sessions and therefore force himself to talk about painful issues. The "good" days were those where he managed not to think about those issues. The "bad" days were linked with "dirty" activities, for example, masturbating and watching pornographic videos. It is impor-tant to mention that, at the same time he felt pain and disgust before certain situations, Joaquín forced himself to make them to have pleasure. We would say then that Joaquín enjoyed with that symptom, the situation that arose in him ambivalent sensations.

As we saw in the previous chapters, the position of the subject of the unconscious is located far from the sense that, from the logic of reason, can be given. In the current case, the reality discovered by Freud operates, that is, the psychic reality. The question is: is it the infantile operating from the unconscious causing effects in the subject, no matter the age? If so, in what way does the infantile in Joaquín appear in the psychic reality to affect the "effective" reality?

The infantile sexual theories have the function of explaining the child of both the origin and something about his existence in relation to the Other, with this we can say that the subject, in his repetition, casts the call to this Other for him to tell what he knows. But we know that this knowledge the subject turns to is the unconscious knowledge, that is, he runs into the impossibility of knowing the whole truth.

Under the logic of the clinic of the interpretation that points to elucidate, the interventions would be based in symbolizing the saying of the patient. This "symbolizing" is frequently more similar to him understanding and having a sense of "why" he behaves the way he does than to the articulation through the signifier.

The infantile, as the sexual repressed, appears in the enjoyment of doing something that embarrasses and, at the same time, becomes the only way to obtain a parasite enjoyment in which is not included the Other sex (the masturbation). Another perspective of this act implies the phantom, since it repays an amount of pleasure to the subject. The fantasy of people masturbating and touching the objects with dirty hands announces the phantom that Joaquín holds in his bond with the others, that is to say, between good days and bad days; those were the crystals where he located the people, and between them, himself.

This way the suffering of the analysand appears at the same time as something searched, or, desired. For this part of our study, we will follow Peusner in his book *The Suffering of the Children* (Peusner, 2009), where he poses that there is a suffering in the child and, at the same time, it is present in the suffering of the Other caused by the impossibility of educating the infant, what indicates that the suffering is not conceivable, but inherent to the culture and that, as a consequence, the treatment wouldn't aim to remove the suffering of the subject, but to ask about the causality of it.

Regarding the suffering, Peusner proposes the Lacanian formula of "For every X, the discontent in the culture has value". This formula turns, in Lacan, to the formulas of sexuation to the phallic universal (Peusner, 2009), with which we can think that our teenager, by being immersed in the signifier net, is also immersed in enjoyment.

But how does he carry this out? Evidently the possibilities for enjoyment in the analysis diversify by means of the transference. However, this panorama that could seem disappointing or far from what psychotherapy promises is part of a movement that the subject himself allows.

Without doubt, the interpretations do not aim toward the obsessive actions, so to make then disappear. The matter at hand is to clarify that the symptom(s) is(are) a guide to unweave that which knots Joaquín's enjoyment that we know is supported by the phantom of masturbation. If we read the symptom, this reading will aim to the question of that enjoyment, never easy to abandon. In that way we can try to locate him in the positions that this young man occupies in the family.

It is possible to think that at the beginning Joaquín's symptom is not that clear, because the demand doesn't come from him, but of what he avoids to find, that is, the sexual trace of the Other. The fantasy that holds and gives sense to the symptom is located in that other register, as we saw in Chapter 2, in relation to the dream and the hysteric symptom. This way we consider authorized to think a libidinal ties between Joaquín's sexual fantasies and the repressed infantile. The question is: how do we locate in his saying – or in his silence – the opening of the infantile while it parts from the unconscious, without trying to locate an "objective" memory, but a discursive flow?

To follow this question, it is necessary to turn to our elucidations about the position of the child in the psychoanalysis, and the proposal of a child as spectrum. For this, it is necessary to locate Joaquín at the beginning of his treatment. This will allow us to trouble the entering to analysis and will give us line to think the cuts in the discourse, the constructions and the appearance of the three Lacanian registers. In this Borromean weaving we will call the subject of the demand the subject of analysis.

I had to break it down

As we have seen in the writing of the case, Joaquín arrives to the therapy office when he was ten years old and he had just recently moved to Mexico.

A neurologist referred Joaquín to me. He came with a diagnosis of attention deficit disorder along with certain immaturity in the psychomotor development and some little troubles to express himself, which required, besides the medication and medical supervision, an emotional therapy (suggested by the doctor). Likewise, the mother described Joaquín as an introvert person, a little isolated and who had trouble expressing what he wanted.

The first six months I received Joaquín in the therapy office I didn't hear a word from him. He just limited himself to moving his head.

When he came back from a vacation in California, when he was twelve, the silence also came back. After a couple of months he said: "I need to talk about this, because if I don't do it, these obsessions will never go . . .".

For the first time I listened to him saying "something" that directly referred to his discomfort. It was when he saw the pornographic website where there were men and children. Since that moment, the computer was left "broken down".

It is important to mention that for this moment of the analytical work, some other important events also happened. For example, in one of the trips to California, the mother "cheated" on the father, and he surprised her in a violent way. Likewise, Joaquín listens to this story through an aggressive argument between his parents, causing him great disappointment, anger and despair toward his mother, besides an important detachment from the father.

To locate his position before the Other and in his story, we will underline Joaquín's phrase, that appears as complement (or pierced by the doubt of the memory): "The website I saw was hideous . . . like men with children . . ."

All the narration he has offered is clear, except when he doesn't know with certainty if what he saw were men with children. The image appears as a remainder, as that object that comes back as excess and doesn't cease appearing.

We have worked the position of the child from various perspectives; one of them is the spectrum one. In this, the child comes to occupy a pigeonhole in the family without altering it. It is interesting to see how Joaquín, if not inscribed in the place of the dead, occupies a place held by almost anything.

This "almost anything" makes reference to the signifiers that hold life in death. Joaquín was in a home where the gaze of the parents was on other places and not on him. This puts aside the idea of thinking Joaquín's silence as the consequence of the change of residence and of language. He speaks Spanish, since it was the language they used to communicate at home.

As to the silence and the place he occupied in relation to the Other, we consider this happens for what Freud called the other scene. And this cannot be thought in the first instance, that is, as something entirely of coexistence, since the fact of not leaving friends when moving to Mexico implies a way of making bonds. He didn't spend time with anyone. So, the effect of silence plays an important role, since it is what holds the analysis during several months, until the encounter with the traumatic of the sexuality occurs in this image of children and men.

About the positions that the child occupies, as we have mentioned, they cannot be reduced to only one. However, Joaquín's position can be rehearsed in many specters in relation to the parents. This supposition, unlike the symptom or phantom, allows locating Joaquín in a limbic place, referring to both parents.

This stokes the questions, with which we agree with Rodulfo, about if the child is desired or not. We cannot reduce this by saying "Desired is loved and not desired is not loved", since a child can be desired for not being loved. We can locate him in this paradox to trouble the question "what does the Other want from me?" And the place that the child occupies in the phantom of the parents. We can think of such a position, from the image underlined before (men and children), in relation with his current impossibility of having a couple and of having sexual intercourse, at age twenty-one, as well as the difficulty of creating a bond with the Other, besides the silence.

These positions are traversed for what we have been locating in the work of Freud and Lacan as the infantile. And not only that, we have also mentioned the existing link between dream, joke, lapses and symptom, in which the four are manifestations of the unconscious; thus, some of the infantile is compromised in these four categories. This way, the position of Joaquín cannot be located in a chronological plane of development, but on the contrary, we must fix several subjective coordinates, and to do so, we have turned to topology.

In this order of ideas, appealing to topology implies a theoretical and clinical need. When the subject is not only circumscribed to the saying, but to what is forgotten after the said (enunciation), it is related to the unconscious. This, in turn, is not inside any place, but it is *extimus* to the subject. The subjective coordinates depend on that said by the parents. It is not a coincidence that he had chosen to study psychology after being in architecture for a while, being these two positions of paternal and maternal order.

On the other side, the position in front of the father is compromised as the identification, because we must remember that what is related to sexuality is presented as dirty. However, it is not all sexuality, but the one that has to do with the masculine, for example, the sperm and the condoms. We can even put in this section the masturbation and the discomfort that it causes him when he has to give in to the impulse.

Likewise, it is necessary to locate the position of Joaquín in front of the demand of the parents. For this, we can think it from the topological order. Let us see the way in which we are going to fix such coordinates via the dream path. The parents, despite living together, have had troubles. Let us remember that just during the treatment, the parents separate as a consequence of the mother's infidelity.

This situation provokes disgust in Joaquín before the mother and detaches him from the father. The phrase that Joaquín used was: "It disgusts me to know that I was born from that body". In this sense, the corporeal is in play all the time in Joaquín, we could say that the real of the body is present both from the imaginary and from the symbolic. To come out of the body implies the act of being expelled. To be born from the body, in the sense that Joaquín refers, makes no metaphor, but it announces the emergency of the real. The body goes from being signifier to coagulate in a saying that makes sign of his birth. Here we understand the absence of movement that the signifier allows referring to the phallic value.

In this cut in which the mother is the focus of that disgust, we can note what Miller says about the body of the human being in relation to the body of the animal (Miller, 2002). The subject *is* not the body, he identifies to that image via the *objet petit a*, that is, what is not reductible of the image, thus, to say that the body is signifier implies an identification with it. In this sense, the human being *has* a body, *is* not a body. Referring to Joaquín, coming out of that body implies inhabiting a body separated from the signifier and inhabiting it as remainder.

About being inside the body, Joaquín narrates a dream where the axis is a basement with walls full of shit. In general, he thought a lot about basements. He told there was a dark basement in his house that provoked in him a lot of fear and scorn. The dream was about his youngest brother, who had moved from his room to that basement so not to be in the house. On the walls there was "poop". He narrated that his brother was also bad since his parents' divorce. So, the only person with whom he liked to be was the maid. During that time the brother didn't want to spend time with anyone in the family so he was always isolated.

It is not meaningless that he constantly dreamt about basements, labyrinths and shit. In those days he said his family was "shit". This went along with the sensation of disgust for having been born from his mother. This type of dream is similar to the one that Freud comments about his daughter Anna (Freud, 1899/1986c). In it we achieve to locate a closer relation to the metonymy than to the metaphor. We could say that in children, the dream disfiguration doesn't operate in such a radical way as in an adult, since it appears almost literal. However, the relationship of the basement with the mother's womb is not that far; however, he didn't associate it that way.

The same way, the dikes of repression (i.e., disgust and embarrassment) operate as those points of "no more" and at the same time they guide enjoyment. At the same time that the subject generates the saying of what he loathes, it cannot stop generating an enjoyment that implies repetition. Such repetition aims to solve the conflict between the drive and the impossibility of direct resolution.

What makes the knot is the image of the walls covered in shit. There it is located the enjoyment with relation to the parents and vehiculized toward the mother. We know, for what we have worked in previous chapters, the relationship that exists between the demand of the Other and the mode in which the obsessive subject positions before it, that is, making from such demand his desire. What it gives as an answer is not anything else than what it is useless to him, in this case, the shit. It is interesting to recover the signifier to which he frequently appeals, that is to say, the basement, such as the relationship that this place keeps with the anal cavity and the passive position before the father. This passive position (feminine) in front of the father locates him before the *impasse* of the identification, having as elements to hold it the professions of both parents and the election of psychology instead of architecture.

Let us remember a breaking point that has to do with choosing to follow in his mother's profession in California. This movement implied the end of the analysis; however, it opened the possibility of continuing the communication with the analyst by other ways that allowed the deployment of another part of the story that came to resignify the previous.

Memory of age ten

Joaquín leaves the analysis to discover something about his desire, what confronts us with an end of analysis in the terms we have mentioned, that is, assumption of the castration, traversing of the phantom (or, as Lacan poses it at the end of his teaching: identification with the *sinthome*). Before this diversity of endings, we will put in the forefront the singularity of the subject to think what is presented as an ending constrainedly singular. Just before exposing the third part of the case, let's review the implications that the ending has with topology.

In the epigraph to this chapter, Borges gives us the needed guideline to address the impossible of the analysis and the dimension of the infinite that can become an analysis with no point of detention. Said in another way, an analysis that leaves the space of the analytical dispositive to make way to another space that we will call virtual.

What interests us is not to account the infinite, but of the impossible of the representation of it. The impossibility has been the role that has delineated the action of the psychoanalyst.

Now, the references to the order of the imaginary don't account for the panorama that the "return to Freud" made by Lacan offers us. Freud turned to models to represent those unconscious processes, Lacan turns to the writing of knot to write the structure. This is the reason why we are obliged to follow Lacan in his incursion, both in logic and in topology.

To be clearer, if the subject in psychoanalysis is smeared and the signifier is only represented before another signifier, the object cause of desire is a lost object. The unconscious is not what is unknown, but what cannot be known. On the other hand, the topology abandons the spaces inside-outside that argue about an internal world and another external. Besides, it underlines the relationships of neighboring, leaving aside the metric and the space of two and three dimensions.

For Lacan, these mathematical properties allow him to think the unconscious, the subject, the drive, the demand and the three registers in a non-intuitive way. On the other hand, in Freud we can locate several schemes that aim to form an almost tangible image of the impossible, which borders on contradiction. Regarding the utilization of these new topologic elements, Lacan says: "it is not a metaphor on structure, but the structure itself". The structure we are referring to is, evidently, the Borromeic.

This conceptualization doesn't lack importance, because even though the cut implies separation, in topology it aims to a new articulation. This way the subconscious can be located under these circumstances.

To continue, it is necessary to resume some ideas that Lacan poses in his seminar *Topology and Time*. At the beginning of this seminar he says: "There is a correspondence between topology and practice" (Lacan, 1978). When Lacan speaks of practice he seems to make reference to the psychoanalytic, however, later he makes a correction of sense:

> There is, despite all, a hiatus between the psychoanalysis and topology. This where I put my effort, in this hiatus, it allows in the practice to do a certain number of metaphors.
>
> There is an equivalence between structure and topology. Is that, the id of which we talk in Groddeck, it is that what the id is.
>
> (Lacan, 1978)

Here we have several elements. The one that particularly calls the attention is the presence of the id in Groddeck. Let us see why this impels us to turn to Nietzsche. In *The Ego and the Id* (Freud, 1986a), Freud says that the I is lived by powers foreign to him. These powers are named as the "psychic other", that is unconscious par excellence. They are referred to as the strange, the foreign; *Es*, in German, the id. Here the reference to Nietszche, since in the footer Strachey says:

> The expression "*das Es*" ("the id"), as Freud himself explains, was taken by Georg Groddeck, a doctor that exercised in Baden Baden. [. . .] In turn, Groddeck seems to have taken the phrase from his master, Ernst Schweninger [. . .]. But, as Freud also points out, the use of the word goes back without doubt to Nietzsche.
>
> (Freud, 1986a, pp. 7–8)

Strachey explains that the expression of Nietzsche obeys to the need of nature of our being. This way, the id can be understood as that place of passions

(Freud, 1986a). Without entering the complexity that implies the being, Freud locates the id as first element in the structure. Currently we can understand that what resists in the analysis is not the unconscious, but in the id, the place of the passions.

Now we can make the same reading of the approach of Lacan about the correspondence between topology and the analytical practice. Evidently, it doesn't refer to the correspondence of sets in which each element of a set corresponds to other element of another set, as the hiatus that gestates the impossibility lies in that part of the unconscious that does nothing else than insist by resisting.

The insistence before which the enjoyment becomes the substance of the being announces the satisfaction always half a drive that doesn't look for objects to traverse them, but to border them and to go back. These unsaying dimensions wrap the *infans* before he comes out of the womb. On one side, it's the real that surrounds him and includes his body and, on the other side, the imaginary that comes to align it by means of the symbolic. The Other and its image are dumped in the flesh to make it drive before the demand of the Other.

At first sight it seemed the knots have little to do with a clinical praxis. However, we consider that the clinic has taken a different ethic statute. Topology, on its side, is a useful tool to read the knots in a rigorous way. But we must consider that it is not about an objective reading of the factual reality, but in a formal way, particular and ethical of reading a case.

When we mention the ethical dimension we make direct reference to desire. This is the text of the pre-text that has been where some have stopped their goings, believing they have contributed with more elements to the psychoanalysis. The text of the psychoanalytical practice would be then the Lacanian topology that locates the desire. With Freud, the desire has been located as motion, that is, as mark. Despite there are differences between the conception of desire in Freud and in Lacan, the intention of absence stays as pivot. Let us see what Freud says:

> Thanks to the established connection, there results, at the next occurrence of this need, a psychic impulse which seeks to revive the memory-image of the former percept, and to re-evoke the former percept itself; that is, it actually seeks to re-establish the situation of the first satisfaction. Such an impulse is what we call a wish.
>
> (Freud, 1986c, pp. 557–558)

Now let us see where Lacan locates the desire: "Desire is neither the appetite for satisfaction, nor the demand for love, but the difference that results from the subtraction of the first from the second, the phenomenon of their splitting (*Spaltung*)" (Lacan, 2009b p. 658). Likewise, in another text he says: "Desire begins to take shape in the margin where demand becomes separated from need" (Lacan, 2009c, p. 774).

In Freud we see that desire is located in the perception of the subject about the apparition of the real need of the body and the way the child tries to solve it, by means of hallucinating representation of the satisfying object. This definition of desire still obeys to the intuitive moment of the child screaming. In Lacan, instead, we can see that desire, on one hand, stays as subtraction of the search of satisfaction to the demand of love and, on the other hand, it announces as what is not achieved to be said by the demand. So, the need, as much in Freud as in Lacan, is registered in the real of corporeal pain.

We have talked of the desire, that is, of the real as impossible and of his obliged topologic dimension in relation to the demand of the analysand. To these ideas we add the problematic of the end of the analytical process. In Freud, this end is also compromised to the end of his life with a certain reinforcement of the I.

In the section about psychoanalytic technique in *Scheme of psychoanalysis*, Freud makes an exegesis about the strengthening of the I, giving this orientation to the treatment. The analyst must assist the debilitated I so that it can bear the onslaughts of the id, the superego and of reality. This is the orientation that some post-Freudians follow. What calls our attention now is the "alteration of the I". It says: "To defeat the resistances is the part of our work that demands more time and the maximum punishment. But it is also rewarded, it produces an advantageous alteration of the I, that is conserved independently from the result of the transference and is affirmed in life" (Freud, 2008, p. 179).

As we pointed out at the beginning of the chapter about the implications of the subject that enters to analysis and the one that comes from it, the bet was not on the side of adaptation. Freud considers one of those implications as the alteration of the I. We think that this alteration of the I have more scope with the introduction of the subject and, to be more exact, with the function of the subject supposed knowing, that in some moment locates the figure of the analyst as Other.

The analyst gives place to the unconscious. Similar to the example that proposes Heidegger with the potter and the pot, it is a topologic relationship that reveals the structure of the emptiness. The potter created the pot around the emptiness. As the analyst signifies, he provides the listening of the analysand to create that same emptiness and incubate some of his desire.

In that sense, we propose to think that an interruption doesn't mark the end of an analysis, since the effects to posteriority and the figure of the analyst are left as the trace that marks the difference in the subject. This is the difference between a subject before and after the analysis. At the beginning of this chapter we said that, once it has been heard, the subject of the unconscious cannot go back to be ignored. That is to say, the subject results affected by the cuts that articulate its saying.

Joaquín abandoned the analytical device. However, that possible ending allows him to be located in front of other possibilities. These new horizons don't imply an adaptation in the sense of effacement of the discomfort in the culture, since it continues, it is the symptom that implies the need of that discomfort, from which one cannot be saved.

Now Joaquín has passed from being a child to be a man. He still makes phone calls, and beyond the reason of these, he makes the call to whom once listened to him and allowed him, in his silence, to create that space for the desire that was blocked by the demand of the parents and the medical diagnostic.

No doubt the analysis as such cannot be performed; however, the material poured into those calls is directly linked to the second moment that we had troubled. It is almost ten years later when the grandmother's computer scene acquires the statute of traumatic. Before he could not take over, perhaps that's why he could not enter that house again.

Between different calls and emails sent, there is one that marks another moment: he said that a weekend he stayed overnight to sleep at his grandparents' house for the first time since that summer event. He said that he felt very calm. He was surprised that he was "too well". He had no "ugly" memories and he was comfortable.

Around those days a memory that he had not mentioned before came, about a visit to the doctor when he was ten years old, more or less the time of arrival into analysis. The visit involved that he allowed the physician to check behind his genitalia to assess his hernias. He told this memory to the psychologist of the university. She said: "that is not normal". From then on he was not well. He thought that perhaps that doctor had made him something, evidently, knotted the memory with the image of the computer, "like men with children". Although he claims to have not lived it as an abuse, the event caught his attention.

During this time various experiences were knotted. This topological perspective is linked with the reading of the logical temporality. At that time Joaquín made questions to his parents about sexuality. Before that, the position of the parents, if we locate it in speech, seeks to free as much as possible the anguish. It would be about the speech of the university or about the knowing, because the parents, before the call of Joaquín, don't have another choice but to answer with knowing. Let us remember what Joaquin says: "I wanted to listen to them! I wanted them to speak to me about that! I didn't want information!"

The request that they speak to him can be read in relation to what we comment as a calling. This calling was not to obtain more information but to know his place as the subject in the desire of both parents. That is, it was a call to the Other. The call to the Other has a close relationship with him "what do you want from me?" and the demand there implied. The question is aimed at being the object of desire of the Other and save himself from being the object of enjoyment. The demand announces "I wonder – I demand". The call presents the limit of the law, in this case of desire, as a point of enough to enjoyment.

We have seen that at the seminar *The Technical Writings of Freud*, Lacan comments the cases of Melanie Klein, whose difficulty was the lightness with which she used the words. What interests us in this comment is that Lacan located the calling as the proof of having access to human reality, which we can now think of it as the knotting of the real, imaginary and symbolic.

Lacan entirely locates the calling to the side of the symbolic, however, this calling also involves the figure of the analyst. Joaquín is always calling the analyst. With this we do not mean the phone calls. It is clear that such an act – in the everyday sense of the word – points to the question sealed by the parents with books, which, through analysis, remains open to make some more. In this way, the direction of the cure does not imply to answer that question, but to locate it in relation to the desire of the Other and make it germinate where Joaquín organizes the memories of that time. The moment in which he is captured by the image of the computer.

To say it with Lacanian tools, that image that comes from the real sexual is presented as something unanswered, what initially captures him and anchors him to that scene in which there is evidence of the non-sexual relationship and the presence of sexuality in the relationship with the father, leaving at that time, as a possible solution, the passive placement before him.

The analyst position allows both the imaginary and the symbolic deployment. In this case, the law of desire holds it outside the failed relationship of the parents, who initially placed him as a remainder that had no other function than being a waste. The location of the analyst in the countenance position of the *objet petit a* allows Joaquin to continue calling to ask questions aimed not to the Other, but to himself, by means of the Other.

The act of not responding to the demand of the analysand with knowledge allowed openness to the unconscious knowing, in contrast to the unconscious as a place or an attribution. To talk of opening or closing of the unconscious invites to the position of the analyst, as formation of the unconscious (Lacan, 1987) to serve as that object which causes desire. In the same way that the transference contributes to the uneven relationship of the analytical device, the *objet petit a* in the repetition of the demand makes desire repeat while it cannot be said.

The closing of the unconscious is offered as resistance when the analyst, positioned as *objet petit a*, seals it in the repetition. Lacan problematizes it like that in 1964, where he makes the separation of transfer and repetition. The repetition, by the demand side, is not exhausted if it is not answered. Or rather, the desire is irreducible to the demand. Transference is not repetition; however, through it the transference reveals the places where the subject passes in the elaboration of such demand. The unconscious that pulsates – opens and closes – invites to think about it in topological terms, since if the extimacy deletes every inside-outside of it, we are in front of a reading of the analysand saying, which points to the symptom and the effect of the real that is of it in the speaking subject.

Joaquín saying gets in response an act which empties of meaning the symptom and points to the repetition of the demand that is about love, to say from the unconscious knowing. It is indeed the unconscious knowledge of the unexistence of the relationship between sexes, since neither in his parents nor in any other real referent does he achieve to locate it. The path points to a know-to-do-with-*that* as Lacan well aims it at the seminar in which he problematizes Joyce.

That is the reason for the intervention that causes misunderstanding and not sense. It will be the task of Joaquin as a divided subject by his object cause of desire, to act according to that know-to-do. Joaquín will assume the lack of ending the treatment. The lack is a resignation to enjoyment. A little more than ten years have had to pass so that the child – now a university man – succeeded in making a call to the difference, via the function of the desire of the analyst.

As for me, analyst, to occupy the position of countenance of *objet petit a* also puts me in the ethical position of dropping moorings and know that *objet petit a*, in addition to being that *plus* of enjoyment, is fall. My ethical position as psychoanalyst is assuming the part of the fault that touches me and allows this end (needed) to be a breakpoint in the chain of Joaquín signifying chain. There will be other areas in which he will solve the life that is supported by the death.

* * *

Giving one more round with the weaving of this writing, a particular question arises: what does our reading put in topology and, at the same time, in the clinic? Answering this question or approaching a possible answer allows us one step further. Lacan, in the 1950s, resorted to the symbolic order (metaphor and metonymy) for access to a reading of the symptom and thus decrypt Freud's clinical building. This showed that the Freudian practice was of the signifier because it offered multiple signifiers. Then, based on this idea, how to think of the case of Joaquin?

As we have shown throughout this chapter, it can be made from the topology, while mathematically the relationship of those two scriptures (Freud and Lacan) has not been resolved. To put it in another way: we emphasize the importance of the Borromean knot as support of the metaphor. This writing must be produced in two ways: mathematically and in its use by psychoanalysis, which cannot be done without the clinic.

The topological reading of the Borromean knot remains being a clinic of the signifier, where it takes body. This body is not that of the image of the Other, nor the one that gives entry to the word, nor is it that body that is stained with the *objet petit a*. It is about the body of the Borromeic rope that gives consistency to the stroke of the writing. The knot is stroke and writing; ties that are named as symbolic, imaginary and real.

To make a topological reading of the clinic it may not be necessary to resort to the knots as representational elements. This point is consistent with the idea of Lacan when he says that the knot is the structure, since the topological reading allows the analyst a place to read the saying of the analysand, in this case Joaquín's. Weaving the story of Joaquín was not the task of the analyst, but of the analysand. And as every singular history is crossed by discontinuity, thus reading through the three registers proposed by Lacan to weave the infantile in that history of the analysand did not pretend to seek emotional stability, nor an adaptation or a development, but questioned the certainties that populated his saying to make of his symptoms (pain) a goal for life and his desire.

Bibliography

Descartes, R. (2008*). Discurso del método*. México: Porrua.

Flesler, A. (2007). *El niño en análisis y el lugar de los padres*. Buenos Aires: Paidós.

Freud, S. (1986a). El yo y el ello. *Obras completas Tomo XIX*. Buenos Aires: Amorrortu.

Freud, S. (1986c). La interpretación de los sueños. *Obras completas Tomo IV-V*. Buenos Aires: Amorrortu.

Freud, S. (2008). Esquema del psicoanálisis. *Obras completas Tomo XXIII* (p. 179). Buenos Aires: Amorrortu.

Kojève, A. (1990). *La dialéctica del Amo y el esclavo en Hegel*. Buenos Aires: La Pleyade.

Lacan, J. (1978). Topología y tiempo. *El Seminario de Jacques Lacan 26*. Buenos Aires: GAMA Producción Gráficas SRL

Lacan, J. (1987). *El Seminario de Jacques Lacan 11*. Buenos Aires: Paidós.

Lacan, J. (1994). *El Seminario de Jacques Lacan 4*. Buenos Aires: Paidós.

Lacan, J. (2009a). Función y campo de la palabra y el lenguaje en psicoanálisis. *Escritos 1*. México: Siglo XXI.

Lacan, J. (2009b). La significación del falo. *Escritos 2*. México: Siglo XXI.

Lacan, J. (2009c). Subversión del sujeto y la dialéctica del deseo en el inconsciente freudiano. *Escritos 2*. México: Siglo XXI.

Lacan, J. (2012). Alocución sobre las psicosis del niño. In J. Lacan, *Otros escritos*. Buenos Aires: Paidós.

Miller, J.-A. (2002). *Biología Lacaniano y acontecimiento del cuerpo*. Buenos Aires: Colección Diva.

Morales, H. (2011). *Sujeto del inconsciente. Diseño epistémico*. México: Ediciones de la Noche.

Peusner, P. (2009). *El sufrimiento de los niños*. Buenos Aires: Letras Viva.

Rabinovich, D. (1995). *Lectura de la significación del falo*. Buenos Aires: Manantial.

Chapter 6

What is a child-specter in psychoanalytical clinic?

In this new chapter, the way to go will be transit through the proposals of the phantom just like Lacan indicates, to locate the child as specter and look into the clinical implications of this positioning. Also, how can this place, from topology, make function of a fourth knot in the three registers?

To begin, we will go to Winnicott and his invention of object and transitional space, as well as the difference that appears between Freud's reading and the one Lacan does regarding mourning and its consequences. Indeed, the Freudian proposal implies the acceptance of castration, whereas for Lacan, it comes together with the integration of the *objet petit a* element that integrates an absence.

If we consider that the child occupies a place in front of others, it means that he or she has a space in the phantom of the Other. For this reason, from psychoanalysis, we sustain the difference between child and subject (let us remember the phrase: "in consult we receive a child, but the listening bets to the subject"). According to this idea, in the clinic, one of the ways in which the subject can respond – as we have worked in the previous chapters – is like an imaginary phallus, as symptom, but also like a *specter*. In other words, the child is given an answer that was proposed by the Other. A distance opens that gives way for the subject to respond somehow. It is in this interval with the empty object that a possibility opens for a subject to appear. Between the pleasant and joyous presence that a child is (and makes) for his or her mother, and the absence of satisfaction of a desire beyond the child, is where the disagreement is produced. This is a disagreement between the failed (but sought) object and the subject that appears there. It is worth pointing out that the subject can only appear as a response to the Other if this distance is produced, which responds to the Other in the interval of the not-all that links the subject's life to the incompleteness of existence. This is the condition for the phantom to be constructed.[1]

The child can take the place of another dead child (or, on the contrary, of another child who is "healthy and with no problems"). This is the position of the child as a *specter*. Here, it is not just about the Lacanian phantom, but in it, the specter occupies the place of the eternization of the Other's demand, stunned by some real where there is no dead to substitute, where the substitution of the dead would be a second course, and somehow the child would unsuccessfully occupy this place. The child replaces the lack here, the pure absence of another dead-living child. The child is desire, but the desire for another child; the child is desired as an extension of another. In this sense, the child is an organ that occupies the place of the transplant of a damaged organ; in this case, the body to which the new organ is transplanted is the family. When the child occupies this place, the frontiers between the dead and the living are moved producing a *spectral child*, or even a *zombie* child, a child dead in life with the life of a dead person.

In Chapter 2 we named this difference in relation to the position of the child in the family. The child as a phallus, symptom or specter. Rodulfo has proposed the triad of the child as a phallus, symptom and phantom, being its coexistence the main hypothesis (Rodulfo, 2006). He defines the child as phantom as the extreme of the impossibility to elaborate mourning, that is, the child that occupies the place of the dead sibling.

The impossibility to elaborate grief, as Rodulfo proposes, allows us to think it with Freud from the beginning of his studies about neuroses. In this sense, Freud did not hesitate to sustain their sexual character. In 1893, in his "Manuscript B", he assured that "The hysterical symptoms that had not been inherited, are [. . .] traumatic" (Freud, 1986a, pp. 217–218). On the other hand, in 1895, in his *Studies on Hysteria*, he continued to look for the forgotten real scene, "Hysterics suffer mainly from reminiscences" (Freud, 1986b p. 33). The cause for this forgetfulness is a real scene and each symptom leads to that designated by Freud as "the lost mnemonic memory". In "Manuscript L", he introduces fantasies calling them "psychic parapets" (Freud, 1986c, p. 289) constructed to prevent the access to memories. This is nothing more than what he would call "primary scenes". On the other hand, in "Manuscript M", fantasies arise from the unconscious combination of experienced and heard elements, fragmented, deformed and linked with a total inattention of chronology: "With it, an originating nexus becomes unreachable" (Freud, 1986d, p. 293) But it is in "Letter 69" in which he would confess – incredulous and at the same time "proud to be able to exercise such self-criticism" – in not believing in his neurotics, since the scenes of seduction told by his patients are impossible to distinguish from those fantasized. Being that "there is no sign of reality that allows distinguishing truth from fiction invested with affection" (Freud, 1986d, p. 302) in the unconscious, it is very possible that sexual fantasies have the parents as protagonists. Thus, Freud comes ahead of the concept of the Oedipus complex.

The proposal that the primordial connection has been lost pushes us to think that there is a more precarious space, even before the substitution-occupation of the place of the dead sibling, which would be the knot for which grief cannot take place. In this sense, grief does not take place because there is no grief to hold: there is no sign of reality. Regarding substituting the dead, the replacement is tragic in itself; however, it is even more complicated when it is not even possible to make that substitution. Indeed, it is a space similar to a limbo where souls do not remain on earth, but do not go to Hell, either. It is about the child located on a grille where there is no possibility to move. There is a fracture, but not a break that allows the child to move regarding his or her parents.

Between Winnicott and faeries

We are in a world that does not finish fading. To say it in different terms, we are facing a frame of the phantom that is held from a fracture, the world of fantasy that does not necessarily refer us to a false world. In that other possibility it gestates the relationships between the subjects; we could say that it even determines them. That is where the child is played. Among the gods, their dusks and their fractures we know of the existence of the beings that do not belong to one world or the other (*The banquet*). In this sense, it is interesting to locate the dynamics that are established in that intermediate world, dynamics of phantoms, witches and other mythical beings, which allow us to think the specter as that which threatens to come back; being the child who can occupy that place.

With the arrival of Judeo-Christianity, the polytheistic world of hordes and tribes moved toward a monotheistic space. From gods and totems, we went, with the Middle Ages, to the invasion of witches, faeries, gnomes and demons, where these faery beings taking to their last consequences represented the limit of otherness; because since then they have been subjectively bearers of phantom images that result from different historical times and discursive moments. The non-human was represented as atavistic, as an unbearable biological remain, and at the same time fused with the human:

> The origin of faeries and all kinds of faery beings (scaled beings, elves, faeries, gnomes, etc.) had an intimate relationship with this moment in which religion and the divine belief towards angels, expressed a complete identification with the child; these supernatural beings had characteristics of incompleteness proper of the infantile condition.
>
> (Stavchansky, 2008, p. 13)

The myth of the rebel angel holds the origin of these beings with a child's soul. It is God who has Heaven's gates closed so that angels do not come out and do not go to Hell. However, there is an angel, the rebel angel who escapes Heaven before the gates are closed completely. This angel does not submerge into the earth to inhabit Hell either, for which he decides to hide in the boundaries of earth. This is how the angel veils his presence mocking God and demons, moving toward the threshold that divides Heaven from Hell, incarnating – due to its small size – the beings we know as faeries, elves and gnomes.

It is an angel, also called a messenger or *daimonium*. What we underline is the characteristic of incompleteness and rebellion with which the child's condition is announced. We face a world located, like the angel, at the borders of the earth. That is, we have a non-corporeal being that inhabits a place that is in itself the limit and the dimension between two worlds. It is a place where the child, as incomplete, can be located regarding God's demand and the punishment for breaking rules. Funny enough, by breaking the command, the condition of the faery, elf or gnome is installed. It is not man, it is not God, it is something else, it is a *specter*.

To locate it, it is necessary to speak about the space between these two earths. Why does it become necessary to go to the idea of a fantastical world and call for the appearance of the specter? In this sense, it is necessary to rescue that space that never stops being a journey and never ends up being a place.

We will take again the idea of transitional space, according to Winnicott, and the specter, according to Derrida. Both authors will help clarify this subjective position. Likewise, it is important to insist that the specter does not contradict the formula of the phantom that Lacan introduced, but it is played in it. The specter will allow realizing that it enables the child to be positioned as a phantom, according to Rodulfo, regarding the parents.

The position of the phantom that a child occupies is somehow a point of synthesis. The question is: how is it that this child cannot be positioned there? Apparently that sort of metaphor is not always achieved, there are instants that eternize the child's localization in an *inter*-place. This *inter*-place is the necessary space between the child and the Other, that is, it is an *inter* space where the child tries to be the space.

The space implies taking a certain distance from the Thing. Indeed, we must place language in-between so as to achieve the alignment-separation movement in which the subject, which falls as remains, manages to ask the Other what it is (as a subject) for ("What do you want?" [*Che vuoi?*]). In turn, the Other does not answer, not because it does not want to but because it cannot. There, in that space, a slot opens in which the subject is positioned; it is the question for the Other's desire that rescues it. This way, the space, as we understand it, is not a simile of precariousness, but a logical need, and not an ontological one. The space generated by the vase – following Heidegger's example – is the container that creates the void, the Thing. Lacan, in his Seminar XIV, *The Logic of Phantasy*, underlines Morgan's law by arguing that the bet of psychoanalysis is constructed in the not thinking and the not being. The best way to grant a place to the subject of the unconscious is either "I do not think" or "I am not", radical negation of the *cogito* that indicates that there is a place that is emptied in this forced choice (Lacan, 1966).

The situation is complicated when the space of which we speak is not inside an object, but an emptied group, a relation of positions, by being the subject of an organ transplanted to the Other to give way to the space. Note that we do not use the notion of desire, that is to say, the desire is there since earlier – even – than the parents. What we are pointing at is an openness that does not allow phallicizing the child.

On his part, Winnicott offers us the proposal on the transitional object, from which Lacan, in his own particular way, takes back the radicalism of the invention. In class 23 of his Seminar X, Lacan talks about the object's yielding, which directly links to the function of the transitional object. He says: "this object that he calls transitional, in this function of the object that I call a cedable object" (Lacan, 2006a, p. 339).

In his next class, Lacan makes a reference to the function of the transitional object once more.

> What is lacking to this first object that we call the breast for it to function authentically as what it is supposed to be in the classical theory, namely the rupture of the link with the Other, what is lacking is its full link to the Other, and this is why I strongly emphasized that its link is closer to the first little neo-natal subject, it is not of the Other, it is not the link to the Other that has to be broken, it is at the very most the first sign of this link. This is why it has a relationship with anxiety, but also why, from the first, it is in fact the first form of, and the form which makes possible, the function of the transitional object.
>
> Moreover, it is not at this level the only object which offers itself to fulfill this function.
>
> (Lacan, 2006a, p. 355)

According to Winnicott, in the child's emotional development, the mother's face is what precedes the mirror (Winnicott, 1979). The child feels when the mother sees him and connects with him. When the child sees the mother's face he sees himself, sees how she sees him. If the mother loses the role of the mirror, the child looks but does not see himself, and the newborn sees the mother's mood and her defenses. If the mother does not react to her child's gaze, she loses the ability of being something in which to see oneself. Therefore, the baby is still not, but potentially from what the mother reflects, since she anticipates the child.

In 1951, Winnicott wrote the "Transitional objects and transitional phenomena" (1984) article that Lacan translated and published in *La Psychanalyse* magazine in 1960. In this article, Winnicott describes the sequence of psychic occurrences that happen to newborns, from putting their hands in their mouths (to stimulate the oral erogenous zone) to the fondness of playing with a special object (to which they become addicted). They are two groups of related phenomena, although separated in time. Besides the oral satisfactions and excitation which that object produces, Winnicott analyzes its nature, the child's ability to recognize a not-I, its location, the child's ability to create it, invent it or produce it, and the start of a sort of affective object relation.

This way, Winnicott designates as transitional phenomena the intermediate zone of experience between the thumb and the toy, between oral erotism and the object relation, between the primary creating activity and the projection. The children's babbling, the melodies sang at bedtime, the use they give to objects that are not a part of their bodies and that are still not recognized as belonging to the external reality, they enter this intermediate zone. They are phenomena that have a vital importance for the baby just at the time of sleeping, by being a defense against anxiety.

In a certain way, Winnicott describes a process of alignment of the subject before the Other, and in the separation there appears this intermediate zone, which is a void where the transitional objects arise; an intermediate zone between the inability and the growing ability of the child to recognize and accept reality. What Winnicott is interested in is the first possession and the intermediate zone there is between the subjective and what is perceived objectively, between the mother's breast and the magically introjected breast.

In this sense, the transitional object has certain characteristics regarding this: it "is *affectionately* cuddled as well as *excitedly loved and mutilated*", (Winnicott, 1984, p. 22) *it is a first possession that can be accompanied by auto-erotic phenomena. Sometimes there is no "transitional object" but the mother herself. This object must not change unless the child changes it, and it is destined to lose its libidinal charge and be relegated inasmuch as cultural interests are developed.*

According to Winnicott, illusion is the main function of the object and the transitional phenomena that constitute the basis of the start of the experience. In that intermediate zone, constant *inter* between the internal and external reality, between past and future, between the desired and the obtained, between what was said and what was meant to be said and that remains throughout life; Winnicott locates the experiences that correspond to the arts, religion, imaginative life and scientific and creating work. This space is part of the development where Winnicott locates the "transitional object", which Lacan refers to in order to talk to us about that "object chosen for its quality of being specially negotiable, of being originally an object of purchase" (Lacan, 2006a). It is an empty object that produces the illusion of an object that could be found and thus complete the subject in lacking.

The importance of this proposal implies a constant *inter*, a not-being without stopping being, a moment out of the temporal tangible present. That is the reason for which said object that the child possesses must cover certain petitions, one of them is smell and texture. This object has to be a reference of the mother without being one. Lacan takes it again to problematize the dimension of the *inter*, moment that *is not never*, and therefore *never stops being* because *it has never been*. This is different to the time of the unconscious where there is an *almost*. This is understood as an attempt of realization set on desire, whose interpretation gives it that corporeality. The time of the *inter*, the time of the specter, is not located there because it is a time of suspension, it is like being in limbo.

By introducing the *objet petit a*, Lacan opens another gap regarding what Winnicott proposed and the transitional object. The *objet petit a* radicalizes and positivizes the space by giving the void a value that affects the order of signifier. Lacan, in his Seminar X, mentions: "Here, it is the substitute (*suppléant*) for the subject. [. . .] This function of the cedable object as a separable fragment, carrying in a way primitively something of the identity of the body which antecedes the body itself as regards the constitution of the subject" (Lacan, 2006a, p. 339).

Lacan recognizes that the *objet petit a* has a debt to the Winnicottian transitional object, without getting to be a continuity of it, and without being a linear repercussion. It is, on the contrary, a moment where Lacan knots what he had been working in his previous seminars with the partiality of the object and the impossibility to locate the object as a satisfier of needs, donating the disparity and asymmetry in the relationship to the psychoanalytical theory.

In short, the Winnicottian contribution to the transitional space with the key of the faeries sheds light on that quite complicated space, of which Lacan sensibly took advantage of, and we allow ourselves to try out the hypothesis of the specter.

The spectral time

The specter inhabits this world of faeries, elves, gnomes. Unlike them, the child in this position does possess a body and lives stuck in mourning. Therefore, we can talk of the disparity in the relationship under the magnifying glass of the spectral because that subject which we listen to, although a child, it also occupies a peculiar place in the family dynamics, even, as a support. But those relationships do not evoke something other than the temporary asymmetry that Lacan mentions at the beginning of his Seminar VIII, where he takes transference as a main axis. This disparity would allow us to place and understand the spectral temporality: the place of the specter as that failed-supplementary that is in waiting inhabiting the slit, which resists time in the insistence of the unconscious. Just like Recalcati underlines:

> A strange religious sect in medieval Japan made burying a live body and its slow mummification an appendix of its ascetic practice. Its followers were called *miira* (*miira* derives from the Portuguese *mirra*, coined when the Japanese learned of mummification practices in ancient Egypt and as an essential component in the preparation of the bodies). The mystic ritual was a radical challenge to death.
>
> (Recalcati, 2011, p. 231)

The body's resistance turns it into a support of the three Lacanian registers, at the same time that it supports subjectivity and, somehow, stops time for others. It is clear that the uncorrupted body *is* not the person we have said our goodbyes to, however, that same body makes the function of the symbol for those who look. Resistance to time indicates the possibility for the return of the specter. The spiritual part, not to say the psychic, evokes a permanence in this world. Indeed, Recalcati continues, "what is at stake is the attempted self-mummification of the subject, the unspeakable design to produce death in life" (Recalcati, 2011, p. 232).

Recalcati observes that the *miira* search for the perfect, uncorrupted body in mummification, the challenge to death. What is important in these rituals is the transcendence both of the body and the spirit. What interests us is the fascination that the cult of the body provokes. Thus, Recalcati knots it very well to the bulimic and anorexic experience. We take this development to locate the dimension of the body with the spectral, thinking of it as that crack of sight on something that is absent, while it is the father who evokes it and places there, in that void a supplementary body to hold a fragile imaginary.

While the gaze is absent from the start as the *objet petit a*, the drive makes the journey in that same arc that Lacan mentions. The gaze makes the rodeo through the void and returns to the starting point with an unfulfilled satisfaction. The gaze is shown in that journey but with a body-object that supplements the more radical lack: an absence of that which has not been mourned yet. What is interesting is that the intention to mourn does not depend on the subject, but on the Other. In this sense, it is the child as a specter who functions as a perfect alibi so as not to make that move.

In common language, the specter indicates a point of unsettling transition between what is alive and what is dead. The specter is the return – always possible and always sinister among the living – of the dead, that ghost of the dead. However, this return is never peaceful, but it introduces in the established order of what exists – in the apparent completeness of the presence – a division, a break, a non-assimilable element, a non-identity.

Recalcati's indications about Marx and Derrida point toward a spectral logic necessary to be able to locate the place of the child as a specter. Taking again the *inter* to which the subject is destined to always occupy in the signifying chain, to be represented by a signifier for another signifier, provides thus a possibility to locate in the Other and, as a consequence, a place in the world. On the other hand, the temporary *inter* of the specter, as Recalcati mentions with the ritual of the body in medieval Japan, is a way to crumble the image of death with a body that does not erode, but threatens to always be so, suspended between the world of the living and the world of the dead; like Olimpia, the automaton who falls in love with Nathanael. It is precisely that illusion of life that calls it, that gaze that summons it; however, behind that look there is nothing, just a body-substance void of history: "the specter is a paradoxical incorporation, the becoming-body, a certain phenomenal and carnal form of the Spirit" (Derrida, 2003, p. 20).

The spectral time implies injunction. Thus, Derrida takes the phrase "*Time is out of joint*" to announce a present temporality that is always discontinuous. He comments that *time* does not only imply time, but temporality. What interests us is that temporality atrophied by fate (an anticipation in fate, like the drama of Hamlet, will also be analyzed in the case of Paulette).[2] Once the story is traced, it is very complicated to make it turn toward a difference in repetition. Even with Dalí, the twist on which the bet was art and not destruction. Derrida says: "The time is out of joint: *such would* be the *primary corruption* of the day of today, or such would be as well, the malediction of the dispenser of justice, of the day I saw the light of the day" (Derrida, 2003, p. 35).

The specter is announced as a threat, it comes from the past to the future with a broken present (*out joint*), which in the end is what is to come. Although Derrida announces it regarding communism, we propose that this threat implies an *inter* that never is, that is where dilemma is. The spectral time is impregnated with the infinite as well as the finite, paradox is its substance.

There is a difference that resides with the return of the repressed that is placed on the symptom. The specter would be a composition in the phantom where temporality is affected by that *inter* that we have already mentioned. This is where the symptoms and actions captured in this spectral dynamics come from. The child in this position of the specter cannot account for the limbo which has trapped him or her, neither in life nor in death. Derrida says: "Like the work of mourning, after the trauma, the conjuring should make sure that the dead will not return: quickly, make all that is necessary for the dead body to remain located, somewhere safe, decomposing right where it was buried, even embalmed" (Derrida, 2003, p. 113).

The problem is that by there not being a body to mourn, only fantasy remains. What is real of the body is not anywhere, therefore, the specter can return. To put it in different terms, the person absent is never gone altogether, the dead is not entirely so. Thus, the specter would remain as a material support of that absence in the phantom.

Specifications on mourning

The child placed in the position of the specter has an impossibility to mourn as a cause. In this space is where the child enters the game under the rules of a certain temporary suspension. Freud had already dealt with the issue in "Mourning and Melancholia" (Freud, 1986e) in which the I gets more interest. The text is centered on the relationship that the I have with the objects, particularly, with the lost objects and its identification with their absence. There is the knot. An identification, not with the object, but with the emptied place that the object leaves, being the libido what tries to grasp it with no guarantee. The duel would imply a recovery of the libido deposited on the object by the I, while in melancholy that does not happen.

The metaphor of the libido as a fluid sort of worked for Freud, since talking about "emptying" and "filling" implied the presence of containers. In 1964, Lacan, although not using repeatedly the concept of "libido", locates it as an organ, more on the side of the real (Lacan, 1987).

This way, mourning announces a particular relationship with the lost object, not as much as metaphors of fluid, but relationships between voids. The voids that we refer to are those of memory, to which psychoanalysis appeals in order to *make memory* and fill those memory lapses, but not with signs and not with signifiers (Freud, 1986f). The memory that the specter exposes indicates that it has not left yet, this way there is no room for mourning. That is to say, the presence-absence alternation of the object gets complicated, because through the signifier, the object can become more present than when it is there physically. The example of this is the father of the primeval horde, where once the father is dead he becomes omnipresent and with more power than he had when he was alive. That is: one was the hated-loved living father and another the loved dead father and place of identification. Another example that takes us to knot the specter to unfulfilled mourning is Hamlet's father, who presents himself once he is dead and asks his son to avenge his death.

In this case it is about a presence that returns. Freud, on his part – and it is the reclamation he insists – reads Hamlet under the view of Oedipus. What is interesting is that Oedipus "did not know" of the crime, however,

Hamlet's father did know that he was dead, but he was not willing to act. In this sense, what interests us is the return of the king: a return marked by the anguish of procrastination. It is evident that the invocation of the specter takes a high toll on the subject, who pays with the only thing he "has": his anguish. So says Derrida: "For even though such conjuring appears inviting and hospitable, since it reclaims, leaves or makes the dead come, it is always joined by anguish" (Derrida, 2003, p. 125). He later concludes: "The specter weighs, thinks, intensifies, condenses within life itself, inside the more alive life" (Derrida, 2003, p. 125).

Knowing that both Freud and Derrida have systems that diverge in several aspects, we consider that a point of concordance resides in the dimension of the problematic of mourning, terrain on which we are founding our hypothesis. The specter returns all the time, because it never leaves altogether; the I identified with that absence never finishes identifying altogether either. To say it more clearly: it is about a failed encounter. However, Freud does estimate an achieved encounter, but who underlines the difference and arises the rank of impossibility is Lacan. On his part, Allouch says: "It is not about recovering an object or a relationship with the object, it is not about restoring the joy with an object in its particular relationship, it is about a disorder in the relationship with the object, of the production of a new figure of object relationship" (Allouch, 2006, p. 205).

We could say that mourning according to Freud is recovering the former state (whatever this means). But with Lacan, the operation points to a difference. Because in his Seminar VI, *Desire and Its Interpretation*, Lacan pointed toward the differentiation being centered on the *identification of mourning* (Lacan, 1959). We would say, then, identification *in* mourning, where the specter does not catch on totally, despite being invoked and located in the child's body. This way, there is something that obstructs the identification with the signifier of the absence, and only that failed presence that we have called the *specter* remains.

It would be a specter not without a phantom, and as we have mentioned earlier, it is not about substituting one for the other. Lacan had already located the phantom as a support for desire, and it is from this that the child will be taken in the position of the specter to be left afloat in front of the Other's demand, at the same time that he or she occupies a place predestined to fail, for having few possibilities to do something with that parasitical joy. The phantom is still the frame for the specter. Like Allouch comments: "The phantom is like a tornado that drags anything that appears around it to its maelstrom – for example, a transitional object" (Allouch, 2006, p. 244).

The most famous case of this position is Eugenio Salvador Felipe Jacinto Dali, better known as Salvador Dali. Dali's brother, whose name was also Salvador Dali, died at age seven of a meningitis attack. Dali constantly mentioned that he and his brother were like two drops of water. Later, Dali pointed the following regarding his brother:

> It is the ineluctable presence, deep within myself, of my dead brother, who my parents had adored with such superlative love that, at the time of my birth, they named me the same, Salvador. . . . Not only did I sleep with the idea of my own death, at the same time that I accepted that he spoke to me inside the coffin in that state of rest.[3]

Maybe what convoked Dali toward creation was to take hold of his name and not the name of the dead, instead of thinking of himself as the "savior" (salvador) of his own brother he assumes himself as another kind of "savior", maybe the savior of an art style. (Two other famous cases of having the same name as a dead brother are Argentinian writer Ernesto Sábato and painter Vincent van Gogh.)

But a child as a specter does not always have the name of a dead child, because we do not intend to categorize "dead child = specter", which only makes the situation more explicit. A spectral child may not have the same name as the dead but indeed be the support of an unfulfilled mourning or, we could speculate, take the place of a dead uncle or a longing for a doll. In any case, the child takes the place of rejection in an impossible situation that takes him or her to be able to live or not, because his or her place is that of hiding death: his or her life is the void.

From this reading we can reflect about the case of Paulette in Mexico. What if the only thing Paulete's parents desired was that their daughter did not live since she was born? Would her death not be the realization of an older desire? If it were so, the objective circumstances in which she died or was murdered do not matter much, but her position in that family. That she died because of a slip-up or asphyxia with premeditation would coincide in one point: the girl lived as dead. In this precise sense, Paulette is Dalí's opposite. While Dalí occupied the place of the dead, Paulette occupied the place of the living, since she takes the place of a "normal" girl without any problems. This place of the child in which only his or her death or inexistence is desired – since that is a desire already – is also the place of those children that are locked up in basements, that are offered to an institution to be educated, or those who are "inherited" to their grandparents so that they have to deal with them.

We cannot definitely foresee the effects that this produces in the future of the subject's structuring. But we do not care much about the future as a prediction, but as what we as psychoanalysts can open as possibilities for the future of this subject. Psychoanalysis is not about making predictions or diagnosis, but readings of the present structure and betting through the analyst's interventions to open unexpected possibilities for the people that come into the office.

The split subject and its corresponding object as a hole is an invention of psychoanalysis, creation that has clinical consequences. We will then add that if psychoanalysis is interested by the enigmas of sex and death, it is just because these are the two points where the subject and the object of psychoanalysis are all the rage. That the object is void and the subject is split means that there is no possibility to name death and sex. There is no signifier that represents the sex and death of the Other. The famous Lacanian aphorism that says "there is no such thing as a sexual relationship" is what points out the impossibility of an object to complete the subject. Our most intense and complicated dramas are ultimately due to this human condition. That is why in his conference, titled "Remarks on childhood psychoses", Lacan affirms the following: "what institutes the entrance in psychoanalysis comes from the difficulty of the being-for-sex, but its exit, is actually read to psychoanalysts today, it would be nothing else than a reformation of the ethics in which the subject is constituted" (Lacan, 2012a, p. 386).

That there is a difficulty for the being-for-sex means that a mother cannot complete herself with an object called the child, but neither can the child become a totality by stuffing the mother's lack. However, the attempts for this to happen exist, and that is why Lacan talks of a "reformation of the ethics in which the subject is constituted". What does this mean? That given that the object and the subject of psychoanalysis are failed, one because it is empty and the other because it is split, there is no ontology of psychoanalysis. There is no structure of the being in psychoanalysis but an ethic of the subject's constitution. In psychoanalysis, there is no definitive way of being, but ethical positions before a lack in the being. There is an analyst inasmuch as there is someone who speaks for him or her in every session.

That is why there is no psychoanalyst being, but a position that is assumed, not ontologically, but in an ethic that reads the child as a symptom, phallus or specter, so that previously unnoticed possibilities surface from that game.

Toward a possible final reflection

Every attempt to close a text in a circular way presents itself as failed. They are, rather, loops that return on themselves with a difference and with no coincidence. This text is no exception. The ending refers to a starting point for new questions that concern the psychoanalytical clinic, so that the analyst's place implies a constant *being*, under the condition that there is always a demand for analysis and analysands that support it. Proof of this are Freud's famous cases, which Lacan guided toward his own statement in the different ways in which each one resolves the relation with castration and the subjective positioning before the Other. In this case, the child as the specter is the inheritance of this reflection, being this positioning the knot that announces and knots the structure.

To finish, we can set out a series of questions to ourselves, which, starting from Freud's proposal and continuing with Lacan's reading, open up a wide range of possibilities to think the clinical consequences of the analytical act in its operation with the three registers. How does James Joyce manage to locate himself before language and the Other's demand, who, being a psychotic, does not break the bond that knots the three registers? Lacan offers a possible answer at the end of his Seminar XXIII, by saying that this support locates him in the *ego*. The question points toward the sense of what happens in the structure, beyond descriptions.

Why does Dora go from being an accomplice to a denouncer? Why does Hans invent his own castration to be located at a certain distance from his mother, and on a different level with his father? How is the phallus played in Hans? And, particularly, in the case of Joaquin, we can ask the question: why does he break the computer?

Which were the signifiers that moved the analysis to launch it looking for its own title? It was not the mother's or the father's, but that in that insistent repetition a difference is achieved, a distance to be affirmed before the Other's demand.

To walk a little further beyond these questions, we can insist on what was worked at the beginning of the chapter. The child occupies the place of another (child) in a supplementary and failed fashion. The child we call spectral substitutes the lack, the pure absence of another (child), whether living or dead. This child is desire for another child as an extension. What we are talking about is the substitution of the lack.

Here is where Lacanian topology has interesting arguments to think about. The Borromean knot writes the structure because it presents the form of articulation of the real, the symbolic and the imaginary. Lacan started from the psychosis to present the error in the knotting that lets the register corresponding to the symbolic free. Each knot is different so that there are as many kinds as subjects, that is where the tidiness of the knottings that appear in Lacan's seminars comes from. This means that there are possibilities of mistake in the knots of the three registers, but there are also ways to *correct* them. This repair of the failures, so to speak, was described by Lacan himself as "substitutions". The substitution occupies the place of an absence, in this case, the lack of inscription of the Name-of-the-Father signifier.

But what reparation are we talking about? It is precise to mention that the term "rupture" does not have a precise antonym. It could be re-composition, reparation, reorganization and so forth. For Klein, for example, this aspect is not an obstacle, since she works in a continuous neurosis-psychosis that characterizes her theory; a linear conception of time-reality. The absence of the *après-coup* allowed her to be supported by the regression-progression binomial, causing a coming and going between the outbreak and the recovery. However, Lacan senses a different structure, which is constituted as a language, with significant oppositions, and it is in that sense that he goes to the knots. It was in the seventies when he introduces the term "un-knotting" to better explain psychosis. With this he admits a dialectic and functional option: "re-knotting", a signifier that bonds with that of "substitution" (reparation of the failures in the articulation of the three registers).

This way, and following the logics of his indications, Lacan talks of the sinthome (Lacan, 2006b) as that which repairs the failure, which is not the same as the failure. The slip in the knotting of the Borromean knot (real, imaginary, symbolic) is the point itself in which the error was produced. The sinthome is what "allows living" by providing a singular organization of the enjoyment. From being a message to be deciphered, it goes to be considered a print of a particular modality of the subject's enjoyment. This change culminates in the introduction of the sinthome, fourth knot that partially restores the Borromeic character of the chain. Then, the specter as a sort of sinthome has the function of substitution, it occupies the place of the lack and grants the possibility to live even though it is like dead or living-disabled.

In his "Note on the Child" (Lacan, 2007), Lacan comments that the child's symptom is found in the place of answering to what is symptomatic in the family structure, adding that the symptom can represent the truth (which points to the unconscious) of the couple. But, on the other hand, he also warns that the analyst's effectiveness becomes difficult when the child realizes the presence of object in the maternal phantom. This way, we would be talking about two operations, one in which the child answers as a subject, and the other in which the child is realized as an object.

It is not the same answering (as a subject) to the Other, as being realized (as presence of object) in the Other's phantom. Just between one and the other the temporary dimension that inaugurates the interval is opened. That is to say, the distinct trace is opened, and with that the passage that goes from the first space that is donated by the Other to the place that the subject builds with his or her answer. This logical order between one and the other makes way for the not-all that links the life of the subject with the incompleteness of existence. In short, *if parents give life, life offers the interval and the distance, but existence is earned by the subject with his or her answer.*

Notes

1 In 1967, Lacan develops a logic of the phantom which he defines as a psychic organizer and not as a formation of the unconscious, since it belongs to the subject's structure to such a degree that there is no unconscious without a phantom. Freud, in "A Child Is

Being Beaten", had referred to the phantom in terms of a grammatical phrase, and its reversions inasmuch as the subject and the object of said phrase. Lacan takes up this idea in several moments of his work, but it is during his Seminar XIV where he specifies his logical statute. This way, the unconscious remains characterized as part of the order of rhetoric, it is about the grammatical structure as a support of the drive. In other words, the phantom are the stories that the child tells over and over again, which point to a truth without sense, inconsistent, hesitating, where his or her saying, which comes from the Other (distance), is nothing more than the structure that hauls the drive's repeated and unending journey.

2 In March 2010, in Estado de México, four-year-old Paulette disappeared from her house. Being a girl with a motor and speech disability, she was not able to "fend for herself" since her physical condition prevented her from moving without the presence of an adult. For ten days news in Mexico were saturated by talking about Paulette and in finding the person guilty of her disappearance. Suspicions from the start were that her parents, separately or maybe together, organized the kidnapping or murder (death by asphyxiation). However, rumors pointed to deception at all times; the insistence itself to turn it into a scandal became a way to "convince the world" that the girl had choked herself with her own sheets in the same bed in which all the reporters taped their note, and where "no one" noticed that Paulette's body was there in the room. Before closing the case, there were several speculations surrounding it, among these it was highlighted that there were political implications and interests, because at that time Mexico was in presidential campaigns and there were several moves in governmental entities.

3 From the doctoral thesis of Pierre Roumeguére regarding the myth of the Dioskuri, Castor and Pollux, in Dali's imagination, the latter affirms the effect that always identifying as "two Dalis" has had in his life.

Bibliography

Allouch, J. (2006). *Erótica del duelo en tiempos de la muerte seca*. Buenos Aires: Literales.
Derrida, J. (2003). *Espectros de Marx*. Madrid: Trota.
Descartes, R. (2008). *Discurso del Método*. México: Porrua.
Flesler, A. (2007). *El niño en análisis y el lugar de los padres*. Buenos Aires: Paidós.
Freud, S. (1986a). Etiología de las neurosis. *Obras completas Tomo I*. Buenos Aires: Amorrortu.
Freud, S. (1986b). Manuscrito L. *Obras completas Tomo I* (p. 289). Buenos Aires: Amorrortu.
Freud, S. (1986c). Manuscrito M. *Obras completas Tomo I* (p. 293). Buenos Aires: Amorrortu.
Freud, S. (1986d). Carta 69. *Obras completas Tomo I* (p. 302). Buenos Aires: Amorrortu.
Freud, S. (1986e). Duelo y Melancolía. *Obras Completas Tomo XIV*. Buenos Aires: Amorrortu.
Freud, S. (1986f). Recordar, repetir y reelaborar. *Obras Completas Tomo XII*. Buenos Aires: Amorrortu.
Freud, S. (2008). Esquema del psicoanálisis. *Obras completas Tomo XXIII*. Buenos Aires: Amorrortu.
Kojève, A. (1990). *La dialéctica del Amo y el esclavo en Hegel*. Buenos Aires: La Pleyade.
Lacan, J. (1978). *El Seminario de Jacques Lacan 26. Topología y tiempo*. Buenos Aires: GAMA Producción Gráficas SRL.
Lacan, J. (1987). *El Seminario de Jacques Lacan 11*. Buenos Aires: Paidós.

Lacan, J. (2003). *El Seminario de Jacques Lacan 14*. Buenos Aires: GAMA Producción Gráficas SRL.

Lacan, J. (2006a). *El Seminario de Jacques Lacan 10*. Buenos Aires: Paidós.

Lacan, J. (2006b). *El Seminario de Jacques Lacan 23*. Buenos Aires: Paidós.

Lacan, J. (2007). Nota sobre el niño. *Intervenciones y textos 2*. Buenos Aires: Manantial.

Lacan, J. (2012a). Alocución sobre las psicosis del niño. *Otros escritos*. Buenos Aires: Paidós.

Lacan, J. (2012b). *Otros Escritos*. Buenos Aires: Paidós.

Miller, J.-A. (2002). *Biología Lacaniano y acontecimiento del cuerpo*. Buenos Aires: Colección Diva.

Morales, H. (2011). *Sujeto del inconsciente. Diseño epistémico*. México: Ediciones de la Noche.

Peusner, P. (2009). *El sufrimiento de los niños*. Buenos Aires: Letras Viva.

Rabinovich, D. (1995). *Lectura de la significación del falo*. Buenos Aires: Manantial.

Recalcati, M. (2011). *La última cena*. Buenos Aires: Ediciones del Cifrado.

Rodulfo, R. (2006). *El niño y el significante*. Buenos Aires: Paidós.

Stavchansky, L. (2008). *Entre hadas y duendes*. México: Gradiva.

Winnicott, D. (1979). *Realidad y juego*. Barcelona: Gedisa.

Winnicott, D. (1984). *Through pedriatrics to psychoanalysis*. London: Karnac.

For Product Safety Concerns and Information please contact our EU
representative GPSR@taylorandfrancis.com
Taylor & Francis Verlag GmbH, Kaufingerstraße 24, 80331 München, Germany

www.ingramcontent.com/pod-product-compliance
Lightning Source LLC
Chambersburg PA
CBHW050521280326
41932CB00014B/2411